WITH ETERNAL GRATITUDE TO MY ANCESTORS

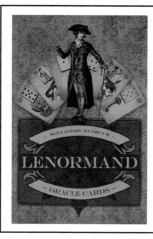

LENORMAND ORACLE CARDS
Alexandre Musruck

- Size: box set 4" x 2 3/4" x 3/4"
- 39 art cards
- ISBN: 978-0-7643-5469-4
- box set
- $14.99

Available at schifferbooks.com

Copyright © 2018 by Alexandre Musruck

Library of Congress Control Number: 2017951897

Type set inMinion & Engravers Gothic

ISBN: 978-0-7643-5468-7
Printed in China

Published by Schiffer Publishing, Ltd.
4880 Lower Valley Road
Atglen, PA 19310
Phone: (610) 593-1777; Fax: (610) 593-2002
E-mail: Info@schifferbooks.com
Web: www.schifferbooks.com

For our complete selection of fine books on this and related subjects, please visit our website at www.schifferbooks.com. You may also write for a free catalog.

Schiffer Publishing's titles are available at special discounts for bulk purchases for sales promotions or premiums. Special editions, including personalized covers, corporate imprints, and excerpts, can be created in large quantities for special needs. For more information, contact the publisher.

We are always looking for people to write books on new and related subjects. If you have an idea for a book, please contact us at proposals@schifferbooks.com.

CONTENTS

PREFACE

"EVERY MOMENT I SHAPE MY DESTINY WITH A CHISEL.
I AM A CARPENTER OF MY OWN SOUL."
—RUMI

Welcome to the world of Lenormand. My name is Alexandre Musruck. I am a professional card reader, card designer, and educator. I have been reading the Petit Lenormand for the last twenty-three years. I first started reading cards at a very young age (eleven years old), using regular playing cards. I first saw the Tarot cards in a James Bond movie—*Live and Let Die*—where Solitaire, a psychic in the employ of Dr. Kananga, describes the journey of Bond as he travels to New York by plane, via the use of Tarot cards. This movie had a real impact on me and triggered my interest in the Tarot. On my quest to discover Tarot, I was led to an extraordinary oracle; let me tell you my story.

It all began when my Uncle George traveled for business to Europe; I asked if it was possible that he bring back a Tarot card deck, and to my great joy he agreed. Three months passed, and when Uncle George returned, I was overwhelmed with excitement. On the very next Sunday morning, my parents and I were invited for lunch, an occasion to celebrate the good business ventures of my uncle's trip to Belgium. I was looking forward to my gift. After lunch, Aunt Claudine presented me with a package. At first glance, my heart sunk; it was too small for a Tarot deck. I opened the package, and I was so disappointed; indeed, what I held in my hands was for certain not Tarot cards.

As I opened the package, I discovered a strange little deck: smaller than Tarot, and my own playing cards as well. My parents taught me good manners, so I simply said "Thank you" with a big smile, and kissed both my aunt and uncle, and did not say a word about my dismay. The deck was called *Le Petit Lenormand* and was named after a woman named Madame Adelaide Lenormand, who was a well-known French psychic at the time of the French Revolution; it was published by Carta Mundi Belgium (and is still available as a favorite to European diviners). I had never seen this deck before, and it was not featured in any movie I'd seen. That afternoon, I sat at the kitchen table to have a close look at the cards. The images were soft, elegant, and quite nice. The little white book (LWB) that came with the deck talked about laying down the entire 36 cards in a Tableau formation, where the reader should look for the cards 28 or 29 (the Man and the Woman cards), depending on the gender of the querent, chosen as the Significators (these cards identify a significant person, object, situation, etc., that is important to the reading), to represent them.

All the cards around the Significator would have a direct impact on the querent or seeker. The simplicity and clarity of the method made me think that the game was more for entertainment, and nothing serious could come of it. Little did I know how wrong I was!

That day, my cousin, Monique, who was doing the dishes, asked for a reading; she and her husband were renovating their house and had just bought a toolbox. A few days later, the toolbox went missing, and she wanted to know if someone had stolen it or if it had been misplaced somewhere. I dealt the grand Tableau as taught in the LWB, and looked for card 29 (the Woman), which would represent Monique. By the cards around this card, it was clear that the toolbox was still in the house—no one had taken it; it was simply misplaced. Then she asked where it was. Through the combination of Coffin, Moon, and Tower, the cards gave me the understanding that the toolbox was up on a cupboard (coffin + tower), in a dark and confined place (coffin + moon). She searched, guided by this advice, for such a spot that the cards had indicated—and there she found it!

As a young diviner, I instantly recognized the practicality and power of these cards. The Lenormand deck came to me as a blessing in disguise, and decades later I am still grateful for all of the wisdom and help that it has brought to my life and the diviner's table.

Lenormand decks have stood the test of time since the late 1700s and remain one of the most popular oracles in Eastern and Western Europe to this day. I always honor this tradition when I create new Lenormand decks, keeping the symbols clear and consistent with tradition. Reading the Lenormand deck today means that as readers we are familiar with the history, while also mastering a reading style that yields practical advice applicable to today's world, even though some of the symbols appear to indicate older, more archaic concerns.

My intention in writing this book is to equip you with unique tools and insights to make you all excellent readers. If you are new to the Lenormand, welcome! I have recommendations to make your Lenormand apprenticeship easier. If you have read cards for awhile, I offer new methods, card layouts, insights, and updated ways of reading for both everyday and spiritual questions that can serve to liven up your readings. My way of reading is unique in several ways: I believe in keeping readings fun, useful, and practical. You will find in my book not only the traditional meanings but added nuances to lend more ways to fine tune your readings to everyday situations. I provide useful advice for each card. I also link card planetary energy, physical, and Spiritual attributes (Archangel energies) when clients want to gain greater insights into the messages provided.

You will additionally find a thorough list of practical card pairings/meanings in the card combination section. All that I offer in this book has been well-tested over many years and thousands of readings.

This book will benefit your readings: I will teach you how to give an accurate and consistent Lenormand card reading for yourself, your friends, and even your clients. Lenormand continues to be an ancient divination system with a powerful simplicity and accessibility. It is an excellent tool for making predictions; the answer is usually quick, clear, sometimes blunt, and accurate, while at the same time, the deck can reply to any question regarding daily events with significant detail. My primary advice to you: Practice as much as you can until the Lenormand system permeates your consciousness. Becoming proficient in card reading as an art form. Let your brain think and absorb Lenormand at every level.

My repeat clients and long-term students who inspired me to write this book remain very positive about their relationship with the cards and the precision of their readings, and are continually finding new ways to utilize the methods that I teach them. This brings me much joy. It is my desire that each and every person using the Petit Lenormand creates love and empowerment with the wisdom the cards convey.

Enjoy your adventure!

With all my love,

Alexandre Musruck
"The Lenormand Extraordinaire"

BEGINNING
WITH
LENORMAND

TOOLS FOR
YOUR JOURNEY

Buy Yourself a Good Deck.

Choosing a good deck is the very first step. A clear, uncluttered deck with basic pictures, the card number, and playing card inserts (i.e., Queen of Hearts) works best. There is a complete selection I've designed for those beginning in the Lenormand.

Consistency.

Choose at least two meanings for each card and stick to them. Make these your foundation. For example, you may choose: Bouquet = gifts, good surprise, Whip = sex, arguments, Stars = Internet, hopes. I do recommend keeping a special notebook where you will write your own repertoire of meanings.

Decide What You Want the Cards to Tell You.

Before framing your question, decide what you want the cards to tell you: Will it be advice, a description of one's personality, or simply a prediction of an outcome? One of the common errors my students make is to mix and match the meanings.

For example, the Snake in general warns you to be prudent. As advice, it would tell you to use an unconventional method to reach your goal; in describing the physical appearance of someone, it would mean a tall, slim, and sexy person; while in a prediction, the Snake would tell you that a sneaky person wants to harm you—beware! Whatever you ask the cards, they will tell you; they are never wrong. It is all about the interpretation.

Frame Your Question.

Clear question = Clear answer! Formulate your question as clearly as possible. Visualize it in your head or speak it aloud, and pay extra attention to the context, as the meaning of the cards and their messages will change with varying contexts.

Journaling.

Keeping a record of your readings is very useful. You can keep track of how a certain card had a particular meaning in one situation, and another in a different one.

I really enjoy rereading my old notebook to see how the reading or the cards held true. It is a way of learning, and this method has taught me so much. In fact, it is largely my old journals that have inspired this book.

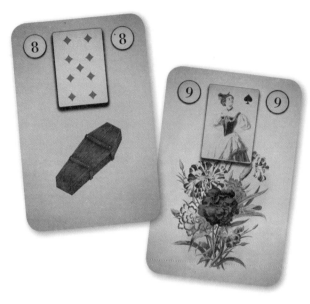

THE
LENORMAND
DECK
ANATOMY

"INSIDE YOU THERE'S AN ARTIST
YOU DON'T KNOW ABOUT."
—RUMI

And now let's have a closer look at the structure of the Lenormand cards. Individually, each card has a central symbol. This symbol is always modified by the next or surrounding cards. The cards are read like pictograms, combining card meanings in a way that results in a phrase that tells a story.

PLAYING CARD INSERT

CARD NUMBER

MAIN SYMBOL

Each card has a different meaning and, again, the meaning will depend on the context of your question; context is key in reading the Lenormand! The court cards from the playing card inserts, present on each Lenormand card, add another layer of meaning, as they can represent people in your surrounding environment or people involved in your question. I will explain more about this further in the chapter concerning Playing Card Inserts.

THE SIGNIFIER, SIGNIFICATOR, PERSON CARD

The two cards that follow represent the querent or seeker asking for a reading. The card you choose to represent your seeker will first depend on their gender. For example, if a man comes to you for a reading, he will be represented by card 28, the Man, and the Woman, card 29, can represent his wife or a significant woman in his life. Conversely, for a woman who comes for a reading, she would be represented by card 29, the Woman, and the Man, card 28, would represent her husband or a significant man in her life.

THE SIGNIFIER CARD

MAN

MALE QUERENT

WOMAN

WOMAN QUERENT

I like to use a deck where the Man and Woman card face each other in direction (see the cards above). In a love and relationship reading, their directional position provides information; if they fall face-to-face to one another or are positioned back to back, this would indicate whether theirs is a harmonious relationship or one of disagreement. These are simple ideas but effective ways of getting clear and quick information. In the chapter regarding Card Spreads, I will talk about distance between cards, known as the Near and Far Method.

THIRD PARTIES

A third party is a person besides the two primarily involved in a situation. In many new Lenormand decks, including some of mine, there are extra cards for Man, Woman, and Child cards that are intended to help the reader in a same-sex reading or when more than one child is involved. Knowing that Lenormand is perfectly structured, the 36 traditional cards are sufficient for these types of readings, but in the case where you want to conduct readings with extra people, I've added three extra cards for Man, Woman, and Child— but know that this is not traditional to the system.

In my technique, when there are third parties involved, I use the Dog card 18 and the Snake card 7 to represent them.

THE SIGNIFIER CARD
GAY RELATIONSHIP

MAN
MALE QUERENT

DOG
GAY PARTNER

A chapter is dedicated to Significators, what they are, and how to use them further along in the book. These cards are very important, as they are the essence of the system, and everything literally revolves around them in your reading. Significators will help you identify the querent's place in a situation, provide more specific details, and help you recognize a pattern.

You can decide to charge or activate a Significator card in advance of the reading.

In a more general reading, the Dog 18 and the Snake 7 would stand for any third parties involved in the reading. For instance, a female sitter asking about her love life may find that the Snake is a rival—the other woman. A man asking about his career may find out that the Dog represents a coworker. The Snake for me will always embody a woman, and the Dog a man. I've seen other readers use the Rider 1 as the male third party, but I continue to use the Dog 18 as the third-party male, because through my thousands of readings, it always manifests in the reading as the male third party involved.

THE SIGNIFIER CARD
LESBIAN RELATIONSHIP

WOMAN
WOMAN QUERENT

SNAKE
LESBIAN QUERENT

THIRD PARTIES

DOG
MALE THIRD PARTY

SNAKE
FEMALE THIRD PARTY

MADEMOISELLE LENORMAND

Marie Anne Adelaide Lenormand (1772–1843) was a French professional fortune-teller of considerable fame during the Napoleonic era. To this day, in France Mademoiselle Lenormand is considered the greatest cartomancer of all time, highly influential in defining the wave of French cartomancy that began in the late eighteenth century and would continue to present day. She gave advice to leaders of the French Revolution and became the personal cartomancer to both Napoleon and later Josephine, a Creole girl who would become the empress of France.

History has proven that Mademoiselle Lenormand did not create the famous deck or system named after her. The Petit Lenormand deck was named after her several years after her death, her name and notoriety used for the sake of a marketing campaign to boost sales. No one knows for sure what she used for her cards, though we know she wrote symbols on them. While we know she did not create this present-day system, it was named after her but not related to the actual cards or images she used.

Mademoiselle Lenormand is and continues to be an inspiration for many diviners. Her tomb at Père Lachaise Cemetery in Paris is a location where many other famous people are buried, including Frédéric Chopin, Honoré de Balzac, and Edith Piaf. Her tomb is frequented often by people from all over Europe who come to pay her homage and ask for special divination gifts.

DEMYSTIFYING
THE CARDS

"You don't have to see the whole staircase,
just take the first step."
—Rumi

Before you start reading the cards, it is important to know and understand the meaning of each card. Like learning a foreign language, one must perfectly know the alphabet and understand the rules of grammar. And here, too, we begin with the basics. On each page that follows in the Meaning of the Cards chapter, you will see that I have framed each card meaning in a way that you link directly to the core meaning for each card. Use this book as a reference by referring to it whenever you feel stuck with a card. I've arranged the meanings so that you can easily find them.

- ☐ **Message:** The message of the card
- ☐ **Person:** Portrays the qualities and personality type
- ☐ **Body:** Body part associated
- ☐ **Timing:** One of the most common questions is "When will it happen?" This section will give you a time frame.
- ☐ **Influence:** If the card is positive, negative, or neutral
- ☐ **Nuance:** The impact of a particular card affecting the querent
- ☐ **Archangel:** The Archangel associated with the card
- ☐ **Planet:** Planetary influence
- ☐ **Zodiac sign:** Zodiacal influence
- ☐ **Love for a single person (S):** Love message for single person
- ☐ **Love for one already in a relationship (R):** Love message for person already involved in a relationship
- ☐ **Health:** Meaning concerning the health aspect
- ☐ **Money:** Meaning concerning the financial aspect
- ☐ **Work:** Meaning concerning the career aspect
- ☐ **Special power:** The special secret power of the card

Please note that I am using the French Lenormand system.

THE CARD NUANCES

Nuance cards are very helpful. They are a group of cards that color the reading and set a special tone for it. The nuance cards are divided into four distinct groups:

- ❖ **Action**
- ❖ **Portrait**
- ❖ **Mood**
- ❖ **Timing**

When one of the groups is dominant in the reading, the entire reading takes on the qualities of the group.

❖ ACTION CARDS
Rider, Ship, Scythe, Whip, Birds, Stork, Crossroads, Key, Fish
These cards' core meanings are about movement, transition, and change. Having them dominant in a reading would indicate that the sitter should perhaps make changes or move forward.

❖ PORTRAIT CARDS
Snake, Child, Fox, Bear, Dog, Tower, Mountain,
Ring, Man, Woman, Book, Letter
These cards are more descriptive; they will color and add personality, giving the reading a distinctive orientation.

❖ MOOD CARDS
Clover, House, Clouds, Coffin, Bouquet, Stars,
Garden, Mice, Heart, Sun, Moon, Key, Cross
These cards will give the reading a sort of vibration, of energy essence, happy and joyful with Bouquet, Sun, Heart, and more anxious with Mice, Moon, and Cross.

❖ TIMING CARDS
Rider, Tree, Scythe, Mice, Lilies, Moon, Anchor
These give a sense of general timing: for instance, Scythe and Rider would be very quick, Lilies with Anchor slower. Refer to the Timing section of the cards for more precise information.

MEANING
OF THE CARDS

1.
THE RIDER —9 HEARTS

Keywords: Good news, Unexpected visitor

Brings good news if negative cards are distant from the querent. The central symbol shows a man riding a horse, showing movement and swiftness. In modern times, the rider can represent a bicycle or a motorcycle.

MESSAGE:
Keep charging ahead.

PERSON:
Young positive man, often a lover

BODY:
Foot and knee joint

TIMING:
Quick, very soon

INFLUENCE:
Neutral

NUANCE:
Action, timing

ARCHANGEL:
Gabriel

PLANET:
Mercury

ZODIAC SIGN:
Gemini

LOVE (S):
Flirtation; nothing really serious, ephemeral relationship

LOVE (R):
One of the parties is keeping distance— probably the man. It can show the presence of another lover.

HEALTH:
Stop being lazy; it's time to use your muscles!

MONEY:
Money is coming in.

WORK:
Something new is on the horizon.

SPECIAL POWER:
The Rider is the bearer of news. Every card that comes before him on the same line describes the message he is bringing forward.

2.
THE CLOVER—6 DIAMONDS
Keywords: Small Luck, An opportunity

The Clover leaf announces unexpected happiness, unless the clouds are nearby, indicating a period of trouble and worry. The Clover refers to a talisman, a lucky charm. It is associated with the color green, the color of abundance and vitality.

MESSAGE:
Think positive thoughts, as they create your future.

BODY:
Good conditions

TIMING:
3–4 days to 2 weeks, soon

INFLUENCE:
Positive

NUANCE:
Mood

ARCHANGEL:
Jophiel

PLANET:
Jupiter

ZODIAC SIGN:
Sagittarius

LOVE (S):
A quick flirt, a second chance, unexpected encounter

LOVE (R):
See the precious relationship you have and how lucky you are to be together.

HEALTH:
Eat more green vegetables.

MONEY:
You can expect a prosperous outcome.

WORK:
Lady Luck is with you, and everything you'll touch will turn into gold.

SPECIAL POWER:
The 4 cards pointing to the Clover show in which area the querent is the luckiest.

3.
THE SHIP—10 SPADES

Keywords: Travel, Vacation, A change

A gain or inheritance is one of the messages of the Ship. Everything related to distance, the sea, movement, or foreign countries. The Ship can relate to your car.

MESSAGE:
Dare to try something new.

BODY:
Liver, bile, spleen, pancreas

TIMING:
Fairly long time

INFLUENCE:
Neutral

NUANCE:
Action

ARCHANGEL:
Raphael

PLANET:
Jupiter

ZODIAC SIGN:
Sagittarius

LOVE (S):
Flirtation, ephemeral relationship, with negative cards, can warn against a liar. Meeting a potential lover on a trip.

LOVE (R):
Consider taking some vacation; travel abroad and enjoy your time together.

HEALTH:
Time for self-care; take a day off; take a trip to the countryside.

MONEY:
Money comes in through business or inheritance.

WORK:
Traveling for your work

SPECIAL POWER:
The cards after the Ship on the same line show where the client is heading or the destination of the travel.

4.
THE HOUSE—KING HEARTS

Keywords: Family, A property

The House stands for many things, first being the family, where you feel at home, the place you feel safe and secure. It's a card of prosperity and happiness.

MESSAGE:
Be yourself.

PERSON:
A good man, trustworthy and stable, a father, a mentor

BODY:
The shoulders

TIMING:
4 days, 4 weeks, a month

INFLUENCE:
Neutral

NUANCE:
Mood, portrait

ARCHANGEL:
Raguel

PLANET:
Moon

ZODIAC SIGN:
Cancer

LOVE (S):
Get out of your house if you want to meet your soulmate.

LOVE (R):
Stay at home today and enjoy an intimate time together.

HEALTH:
Rest; have a nap.

MONEY:
Money coming through a family member, an acquisition

WORK:
Home office, working at home

SPECIAL POWER:
The card below the House shows its foundation.

5.
THE TREE—7 HEARTS
Keyword: Health, Growth

The Tree, standing tall, speaks about your health and your well-being. As you can guess, when surrounded with positive cards, your health is vibrant and strong, and with negative cards you can expect poor health.

MESSAGE:
Ground yourself through meditation.

BODY:
Health in general

TIMING:
9–12 months

INFLUENCE:
Neutral

NUANCE:
Timing

ARCHANGEL:
Raphael

PLANET:
Saturn

ZODIAC SIGN:
Capricorn

LOVE (S):
You can expect a healthy relationship; a long-term one.

LOVE (R):
A feeling of well-being; you know that your relationship is well-rooted and will last.

HEALTH:
You enjoy strong and good health.

MONEY:
Your investments are growing.

WORK:
You will soon harvest the fruit of your labor.

SPECIAL POWER:
The card below the Tree at it roots shows where the issue comes from, and the card above (on the branches) shows where the issue is progressing.

6.
THE CLOUDS—KING CLUBS
Keywords: Confusion, Illusion

Here you meet the Clouds, one of the negative cards in the Lenormand deck. When the Clouds appear, stop doing what you are doing, as you are lacking clarity.

MESSAGE:
Detach from the situation.

PERSON:
An elderly man with unbalanced character

BODY:
Lungs, the respiratory system

TIMING:
Autumn

INFLUENCE:
Negative

NUANCE:
Mood

ARCHANGEL:
Michael

PLANET:
Neptune

ZODIAC SIGN:
Pisces

LOVE (S):
You will meet a man that is always confused—one who tends to make a lot of conclusions without any evidence.

LOVE (R):
You are facing a dark time; don't rush into any decision.

HEALTH:
Stop smoking. Keep positive thoughts.

MONEY:
Don't invest as yet; pay attention to your account.

WORK:
A dark time for work; stay patient.

SPECIAL POWER:
The Clouds darkens all the cards that had come before it.

7.
THE SNAKE—QUEEN CLUBS
Keywords: Jealousy, Manipulation

The Snake is a card indicating danger. It indicates people or situations that are potentially harmful. Be careful who you trust.

MESSAGE:
Pay attention to the people around you.

PERSON:
Experienced cunning woman, the other woman, a third party

BODY:
Large intestine

TIMING:
7 days, 7 weeks

INFLUENCE:
Negative

NUANCE:
Portrait

ARCHANGEL:
Michael

PLANET:
Moon

ZODIAC SIGN:
Cancer

LOVE (S):
You will date a seductive, dangerous woman, a predator.

LOVE (R):
Try something different; break the routine.

HEALTH:
Pay attention; you may have contracted a virus or hidden disease.

MONEY:
Money slips through your fingers; don't lend money to anyone.

WORK:
Dangerous coworker, one who would betray you without hesitation

SPECIAL POWER:
The card that the head of the Snake points to is the one that describes the betrayal and danger. The snake has the power to compel people and make them his puppet.

8.
THE COFFIN—9 DIAMONDS
Keywords: Misfortune, Death

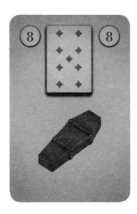

The Coffin talks about sickness, loss, and painful transformation. With positive cards around it, the influence of the coffin diminishes.

MESSAGE:
It's time to rest.

BODY:
Disease in general

TIMING:
Eternity, very long time

INFLUENCE:
Negative

NUANCE:
Mood

ARCHANGEL:
Azrael

PLANET:
Pluto

ZODIAC SIGN:
Scorpio

LOVE (S):
You will stay single for a long time.

LOVE (R):
Your relationship is dying.

HEALTH:
Make an appointment for a checkup.

MONEY:
Money saved, money buried

WORK:
Leaving a job, getting fired

SPECIAL POWER:
The Coffin darkens and kills the cards that come after it.

9.
THE BOUQUET—QUEEN SPADES
Keywords: Gift, Declaration

The Bouquet of flowers signifies great happiness and a pleasant surprise. Your relationships are harmonious; your work is acknowledged; your loved ones are happy.

MESSAGE:
Show gratitude.

PERSON:
Kind, beautiful, and smart woman, probably single

BODY:
Allergies

TIMING:
Spring

INFLUENCE:
Positive

NUANCE:
Mood

ARCHANGEL:
Jophiel

PLANET:
Jupiter

ZODIAC SIGN:
Sagittarius

LOVE (S):
A charming lover is on the way to you.

LOVE (R):
Nice surprise is on the horizon; expect a gift.

HEALTH:
Good and vibrant health

MONEY:
Unexpected income

WORK:
Acknowledgment and compliments

SPECIAL POWER:
The Bouquet on the right-hand side of the significant shows a grateful and positive person; on the left-hand side, the querent is selfish and is never satisfied.

10.
THE SCYTHE—JACK DIAMONDS
Keywords: Danger, A break

The Scythe announces a danger unless positive cards are nearby to soften it. You can have more details from the surrounding cards.

MESSAGE:
Clear away the clutter.

PERSON:
A young man, sometime aggressive

BODY:
Teeth

TIMING:
Sudden and unexpected, very quick

INFLUENCE:
Negative

NUANCE:
Action, timing

ARCHANGEL:
Jophiel

PLANET:
Pluto

ZODIAC SIGN:
Scorpio

LOVE (S):
Your loneliness is reaching its end.

LOVE (R):
A breakup, a divorce

HEALTH:
A surgery

MONEY:
Difficult times are over.

WORK:
Be smart, swift, and decide once for all.

SPECIAL POWER:
The Scythe cuts everything that comes before it, discarding away the positive effect of the good cards.

11.
THE WHIP—JACK CLUBS
Keyword: Argument, Vengeance

Family trouble and quarrels are shown with the Whip. The energy predicts a conflict and aggressive tension. The Whip is a card of revenge, and I have found that in a relationship question, it can indicate that one of the parties feels that they are being punished for something.

MESSAGE:
Choose to be peaceful.

PERSON:
Argumentative young man

BODY:
Muscles, tendons, the penis

TIMING:
11 days or weeks, November

INFLUENCE:
Negative

NUANCE:
Action

ARCHANGEL:
Chamuel

PLANET:
None

ZODIAC SIGN:
None

LOVE (S):
Sex-oriented relationship

LOVE (R):
Arguments, sex, violence

HEALTH:
Muscular pain

MONEY:
Hard times with money

WORK:
Working hard, restarting again and again

SPECIAL POWER:
The cards surrounding the Whip show the area that needs decluttering.

12.
THE BIRDS—7 DIAMONDS

Keywords: Communication, The couple, Gossip, Conspiracy

The core meaning of the Birds is communication—verbal kinds principally! Other meanings of this card include gossip, migration, short difficulty, a couple, and something that involves more than one person. Think of the Birds card as real birds in real life and how they act; use these attributes in your card meaning.

MESSAGE:
Speak your truth.

BODY:
Nerves, throat

TIMING:
Anywhere from 12 days
to a year, December

INFLUENCE:
Neutral

NUANCE:
Action

ARCHANGEL:
Gabriel

PLANET:
Uranus

ZODIAC SIGN:
Aquarius

LOVE (S):
A free relationship, short
term

LOVE (R):
Lots of talking going on,
a lot of sharing, a
soul-mate relationship

HEALTH:
Need a break from noisy
environment

MONEY:
A phone call or a
conversation can bring in
money.

WORK:
Lots of negotiation going
around

SPECIAL POWER:
The card next to the Birds
represents its voice, the
message the birds want to
transmit.

13.
THE CHILD—JACK SPADES
Keyword: Innocence, Small

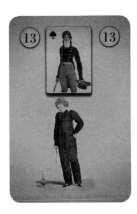

Here is the Child, a sign of new beginnings and a fresh start. People around you are loving and of good nature. The Child also indicates something that is starting small.

MESSAGE:
Be playful.

PERSON:
A young, naïve, immature man

BODY:
Vagina and reproductive organs

TIMING:
A year

INFLUENCE:
Neutral

NUANCE:
Portrait

ARCHANGEL:
Gabriel

PLANET:
Sun

ZODIAC SIGN:
Leo

LOVE (S):
You will start a new relationship soon.

LOVE (R):
You are in a relationship where you truly trust each other.

HEALTH:
Childhood disease, small infection or allergy

MONEY:
Small sum of money

WORK:
Light atmosphere, starting something new

SPECIAL POWER:
The Child card can represent an infant.

14.
THE FOX—9 CLUBS
Keywords: Falsehood, A trap

Be wise and watch your surroundings, as cunning people are hiding nearby. Pay attention to those using flattery and manipulation to attain their goals. I personally use the Fox as my main job card.

MESSAGE:
You have the power to change this situation.

BODY:
Nose, ears, eyes, sinus

TIMING:
2 weeks

INFLUENCE:
Negative

NUANCE:
Portrait

ARCHANGEL:
Chamuel

PLANET:
Pluto

ZODIAC SIGN:
Scorpio

LOVE (S):
Meeting someone who uses flattery to seduce, someone wearing a mask

LOVE (R):
One of the parties is playing a game, hiding their real motives.

HEALTH:
Seek another diagnosis, change practitioners.

MONEY:
Money comes in through work.

WORK:
Be wise and clever; think outside of the box.

SPECIAL POWER:
The closer the Fox, the clever/smarter the querent. The Fox is the master of lies and disguise—beware!

15.
THE BEAR—10 CLUBS

Keywords: Strength, Something big

Keep your distance from people you know who are envious of your happiness. The Bear is a card of finances, as it can represent a large sum of money with positive cards. I personally use the Bear as one of my money cards.

MESSAGE:
Take back your powers.

PERSON:
A protective mother

BODY:
Eating disorders

TIMING:
2 weeks, between 6 to 8 months

INFLUENCE:
Neutral

NUANCE:
Portrait

ARCHANGEL:
Gabriel and Michael

PLANET:
Mars

ZODIAC SIGN:
Aries

LOVE (S):
Believe in yourself, and be yourself.

LOVE (R):
Temper your aggressiveness.

HEALTH:
Pay attention to what you eat.

MONEY:
A large sum of money comes your way.

WORK:
Your boss acknowledges your tenacity and hard work.

SPECIAL POWER:
The closer the Bear, the stronger the querent.

16.
THE STARS—6 HEARTS
Keywords: Hope, Guidance

The Stars is a sign of hope, confirming that you are on the right path; pray that the clouds are far, as they can alter your fortune from a bright one to a dark one. I use the Stars as my card for networking.

MESSAGE:
Make a wish.

BODY:
The skin

TIMING:
At night, 2 weeks

INFLUENCE:
Positive

NUANCE:
Mood

ARCHANGEL:
Uriel

PLANET:
Neptune

ZODIAC SIGN:
Pisces

LOVE (S):
Let them know that you are accessible.

LOVE (R):
Romantic evening

HEALTH:
An expansion of a disease or infection

MONEY:
Money comes in through recognition and rewards.

WORK:
The show business, entertainment industry; use your talent.

SPECIAL POWER:
The Stars have the power to magnify things. With positive cards around, you can expect a miracle; with strong negative cards, it announces misfortune.

17.
THE STORK—QUEEN HEARTS
Keywords: Movement, Change

The Stork indicates some kind of change coming, like a pregnancy or a relocation. It's a good omen to have the Stork near as an upgrade; a positive change or job promotion can be expected.

MESSAGE:
Raise your standards.

PERSON:
Sweet and loving woman

BODY:
The legs

TIMING:
Spring, 17 days

INFLUENCE:
Positive

NUANCE:
Action

ARCHANGEL:
Gabriel

PLANET:
Mercury

ZODIAC SIGN:
Gemini

LOVE (S):
A change is announced; use this opportunity to meet someone new or someone you love.

LOVE (R):
Happy life changes, unexpected pregnancy

HEALTH:
An upgrade; things are doing better.

MONEY:
Money gain through a promotion or a raise in salary

WORK:
Successful business with foreign partners

SPECIAL POWER:
The cards after the Stork on the same line show where the client is heading or the destination of his relocation.

18.
THE DOG—10 HEARTS
Keywords: Friendship, A partner

The Dog indicates a loyal and trustworthy friend, someone
you can count on in any circumstance. With the Dog, you
have an ally; you are protected. I sometimes see the Dog
as a protector, a guardian angel.

MESSAGE:
You are guided and
protected.

PERSON:
A young man, the other
man, a third party

BODY:
The tongue, the nose,
sinus

TIMING:
18 days, the 18th of a
month

INFLUENCE:
Positive

NUANCE:
Portrait

ARCHANGEL:
Raguel, your guardian
angel

PLANET:
Uranus

ZODIAC SIGN:
Aquarius

LOVE (S):
You will meet a
trustworthy and loyal
partner.

LOVE (R):
Your love is protected,
with nothing to fear.

HEALTH:
Your health is protected.

MONEY:
Money comes to you via
friends and trusted
business partners.

WORK:
Collaborating with a
friendly and loyal
colleague

SPECIAL POWER:
The Dog is a shield; it has
the power to protect the
querent from the
influence of negative
cards if it stands near
him.

19.
THE TOWER—6 SPADES

Keyword: Isolation, Security, The past

The Tower is a tall building; it can indicate a school,
hospital, or government building, depending on the surrounding
cards. In a more general way, the Tower is calling you to raise
your standards and to maintain healthy boundaries; don't
let anyone invade your peacefulness.

MESSAGE:
Build healthy boundaries.

BODY:
The spine

TIMING:
19 days, the 19th of a
month

INFLUENCE:
Neutral

NUANCE:
Portrait

ARCHANGEL:
Michael

PLANET:
Saturn

ZODIAC SIGN:
Capricorn

LOVE (S):
You need to leave this
state of solitude.

LOVE (R):
This relationship is
lifelong.

HEALTH:
Depression, mental
illness

MONEY:
Money saved, money in
the bank

WORK:
You are reaching a
significant milestone.

SPECIAL POWER:
The Tower has the power
to structure and put
things in order.

20.
THE GARDEN—8 SPADES

Keyword: A gathering, An invitation

The Garden announces that you will soon be introduced to a group of people, and a new friendship will be born. You will be invited to a birthday, wedding, gathering, or a party.

MESSAGE:
It's time to make new friends.

BODY:
Immune system

TIMING:
20 days, 20th of a month

INFLUENCE:
Neutral, positive

NUANCE:
Portrait, mood

ARCHANGEL:
Raguel

PLANET:
Uranus

ZODIAC SIGN:
Aquarius

LOVE (S):
It's party time! You need to go out more.

LOVE (R):
Your relationship is reaching an important level.

HEALTH:
Good health

MONEY:
Money gain through successful enterprise

WORK:
Teamwork

SPECIAL POWER:
The Garden has the power to create warm ambiance and in no time make a party from nothing.

21.
THE MOUNTAIN—8 CLUBS

Keyword: Obstacle, An Uphill Climb

The Mountain warns of an obstacle or an enemy that may be blocking your progression. You will need to make great efforts to overcome the Mountain's energy.

MESSAGE:
Stand your ground and persevere!

BODY:
The head

TIMING:
21 days, the 21st of a month

INFLUENCE:
Negative

NUANCE:
Portrait

ARCHANGEL:
Michael

PLANET:
Mars

ZODIAC SIGN:
Aries

LOVE (S):
Staying single; a past relationship issue is keeping you from moving forward.

LOVE (R):
You are experiencing some sort of blockage and standstill.

HEALTH:
The need to rest

MONEY:
Nothing on the horizon for now

WORK:
Hard work, a complicated task

SPECIAL POWER:
The Mountain has the power to make things heavy and difficult to move.

22.
THE CROSSROADS
—QUEEN DIAMONDS

Keyword: Choice, Decision

The time has come for you to make a decision, as you are at an important crossroad. Two options are offered to you; choose wisely!

MESSAGE:
Decide now.

PERSON:
An energetic woman

BODY:
Arteries, veins, lymphatic channels

TIMING:
From 2 days to 2 months, February

INFLUENCE:
Neutral

NUANCE:
Action

ARCHANGEL:
Uriel

PLANET:
Venus

ZODIAC SIGN:
Libra

LOVE (S):
It's decision time; consider carefully.

LOVE (R):
You need to review and decide in which direction you want to take your relationship.

HEALTH:
A decision needs to be made.

MONEY:
A wise decision may pay off.

WORK:
Choose the one that suits your qualifications.

SPECIAL POWER:
The Crossroads always point to two options; before taking any decision, see which 2 cards (1 top and 1 bottom) are perpendicular to the Crossroads to help you with your decision-making.

23.
THE MICE—7 CLUBS

Keyword: Stress, Loss, Payments

The Mice predict a stressful situation; something may be taken away from you. Ask the surrounding cards what that might be—the further the Mice are from the Significator, the more unlikely the recovery of the loss.

MESSAGE:
Let go.

BODY:
Small intestine, stomach

TIMING:
Very fast; minutes, hours, less than a month

INFLUENCE:
Negative

NUANCE:
Mood

ARCHANGEL:
Azrael, Chamuel

PLANET:
Saturn

ZODIAC SIGN:
Libra

LOVE (S):
Stress regarding your celibacy

LOVE (R):
Stress regarding your relationship

HEALTH:
Cancer, anxiety, disease, or worry that eats away at you

MONEY:
Loss and ruin

WORK:
Stressful coworker and atmosphere

SPECIAL POWER:
The mice have the power to eat things away; after a series of unfortunate cards, you can expect good things to happen as the negativity is eaten away.

24.
THE HEART—JACK HEARTS
Keyword: Feeling, Emotion

The Heart speaks about your true desires and feelings regarding your question. The Heart assures that you are loved and cherished if surrounded by positive cards.

MESSAGE:
Follow your passion and love yourself.

PERSON:
Young and positive man

BODY:
Heart, blood circulation

TIMING:
Spring, Summer, February

INFLUENCE:
Positive

NUANCE:
Mood

ARCHANGEL:
Raphael

PLANET:
Sun

ZODIAC SIGN:
Leo

LOVE (S):
You can expect to meet your soulmate.

LOVE (R):
You are sharing an emotional, romantic time.

HEALTH:
Love your body; take care of your heart.

MONEY:
Financial stability

WORK:
You are doing a job that you love.

SPECIAL POWER:
The heart has the power to make people fall in love.

25.
THE RING –ACE CLUBS
Keyword: Commitment, Deal

The Ring represents your committed relationship, or a wedding. It represents an affirmation, a confirmation, a "yes" answer. Happy is the single lady who has the ring near the bouquet.

MESSAGE:
Go for it.

BODY:
Chronic disease

TIMING:
A significant date for the querent, such as an anniversary

INFLUENCE:
Positive

NUANCE:
Portrait

ARCHANGEL:
Raphael

PLANET:
Venus

ZODIAC SIGN:
Libra

LOVE (S):
You will soon be in a committed relationship.

LOVE (R):
Your relationship is reaching the next level.

HEALTH:
Commit to a healthy lifestyle.

MONEY:
Money comes in through deals and contracts.

WORK:
A business deal, a contract

SPECIAL POWER:
The ring has the amazing power of binding and committing people to cause and situation.

26.
THE BOOK—10 DIAMONDS
Keyword: Secret, Unknown information

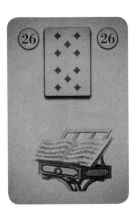

The Book tells us that a secret is hidden in this situation. Look at the cards surrounding the Book, as they will break the seal and reveal the secret.

MESSAGE:
Silence is golden.

BODY:
The unconscious

TIMING:
Unknown

INFLUENCE:
Neutral

NUANCE:
Portrait

ARCHANGEL:
Metatron

PLANET:
Neptune

ZODIAC SIGN:
Pisces

LOVE (S):
A secret relationship, a hidden secret

Love (L): You are discovering each other and learning much about your relationship.

HEALTH:
A health issue may be unknown at the moment.

MONEY:
Your bank account, hidden money

WORK:
Learning more, secret deal

SPECIAL POWER:
The Book has the power to mask things; what you think you know may not be!

27.
THE LETTER—7 SPADES
Keyword: Information, Document

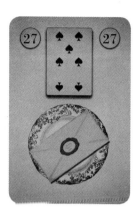

The Letter appears when written information is coming toward the querent. Depending on the surrounding cards, the news can be good or bad, and these will also give more clues on the nature of the correspondence.

MESSAGE:
Pour your heart out.

BODY:
Hands and fingers

TIMING:
27th of a month

INFLUENCE:
Neutral

NUANCE:
Portrait

ARCHANGEL:
Gabriel

PLANET:
Mercury

ZODIAC SIGN:
Gemini

LOVE (S):
A love letter, a message of love

LOVE (R):
A love letter, a message of love

HEALTH:
Result of a checkup, a prescription

MONEY:
A check

WORK:
A contract, work-related information

SPECIAL POWER:
Words are some of the most powerful forces on earth; use them wisely!

28.
THE MAN—ACE HEARTS
Keyword: Partner, Husband

The Man card represents the male querent asking for the reading; the cards around it will have a direct impact on his situation.

MESSAGE:
Connect with your masculine energy.

PERSON:
Young and positive man

INFLUENCE:
Neutral

ANGEL:
Guardian Angel

PLANET:
Mars

ZODIAC SIGN:
Aries

LOVE (S):
A potential lover, soulmate

LOVE (R):
Your husband, an important man

HEALTH:
Take charge.

MONEY:
Create your own prosperity.

WORK:
You are a leader.

29.
THE WOMAN—ACE SPADES
Keyword: Partner, Wife

The Woman card represents the female asking for the reading; the cards around it will have a direct impact.

MESSAGE:
Connect with your feminine energy.

PERSON:
Young and positive woman

INFLUENCE:
Neutral

ANGEL:
Guardian Angel

PLANET:
Venus

ZODIAC SIGN:
Taurus

LOVE (S):
A potential lover, soulmate

LOVE (R):
Your wife, an important woman

HEALTH:
Take charge.

MONEY:
Create your own prosperity.

WORK:
You are a leader.

30.
THE LILIES—KING SPADES
Keyword: Honesty, Integrity

The Lilies on top of the querent testifies to his/her honesty and loyalty, but if this card falls below the querent in a spread, it is a sign of falseness and dishonesty. Lilies are also a symbol of high honor, the fleur-de-lis being the symbol of the French monarchy.

MESSAGE:
Patience please!

PERSON:
Distinguished elder man

BODY:
Alzheimer's disease,
age-related disease

TIMING:
Winter

INFLUENCE:
Neutral

NUANCE:
Timing

ARCHANGEL:
Gabriel

PLANET:
Moon

ZODIAC SIGN:
Virgo

LOVE (S):
You will meet an elderly
partner.

LOVE (R):
You will be experiencing
a moment of joy and
happiness.

HEALTH:
Take some rest.

MONEY:
Be cautious and patient.

WORK:
Peace and serenity is
yours.

SPECIAL POWER:
The Lilies card has the
power to bring peace and
serenity to any situation.

31.
THE SUN—ACE DIAMONDS
Keyword: Joy, Success

The Sun card is always an auspicious card in a reading. As the Sun shines brightly near the querent, he can expect his troubles and worries to disappear. The presence of the Sun near negative cards will burn their negative influence away and shed immense blessings on the situation.

MESSAGE:
Let your light shine.

ARCHANGEL:
Uriel

HEALTH:
Good and vibrant health

BODY:
Physical appearance

PLANET:
Sun

MONEY:
New source of income

TIMING:
Summer, in the morning, daytime

ZODIAC SIGN:
Leo

WORK:
Success is yours, working in a positive atmosphere

LOVE (S):
Lots of openings, a chance to meet the right person

INFLUENCE:
Positive

SPECIAL POWER:
The Sun has the power to expose things to the light: good or bad.

NUANCE:
Mood

LOVE (R):
Happy times together

32.
THE MOON—8 HEARTS
Keyword: Reputation, Intuition

The Moon by your side foretells that fame and honor is yours in any of your ventures; your creativity and work are being acknowledged. It's a time that you should appreciate and use to open new doors.

MESSAGE:
Dream big

BODY:
Menstrual cycle, the womb, menopause

TIMING:
Evening, moon cycle

INFLUENCE:
Positive

NUANCE:
Mood

ARCHANGEL:
Haniel

PLANET:
Moon

ZODIAC SIGN:
Cancer

LOVE (S):
A romantic partner is coming forward.

LOVE (R):
Romantic time spent together

HEALTH:
Doubts and worries, lunatic

MONEY:
Manage your budget wisely.

WORK:
Pay attention to your intuition.

SPECIAL POWER:
The Moon has the power to heighten your intuition.

33.
THE KEY—8 DIAMONDS

Keyword: Success, Solution

If you have the Key in your possession, nothing wrong can happen. Near you, you have the power to take charge and handle any situation. The Key points to the solution to a problem; notice the surrounding cards.

MESSAGE:
Go for it!

BODY:
The Chakras

TIMING:
Now

INFLUENCE:
Positive

NUANCE:
Portrait, action, mood

ARCHANGEL:
Gabriel

PLANET:
Venus

ZODIAC SIGN:
Taurus

LOVE (S):
This is the right partner.

LOVE (R):
You will succeed in everything; this relationship is significant.

HEALTH:
Nothing to worry about

MONEY:
Solutions and a new door to prosperity appear before you.

WORK:
Work is easy and meaningful.

SPECIAL POWER:
The Key has the power to unlock all kinds of doors.

34.
THE FISH—KING DIAMONDS
Keyword: Money, Business exchange, Transaction

The Fish near the querent foretells successful enterprises. I always see the Fish when I will be investing in some sort of project or purchase. It is a card of abundance and fertility, and can reinforce the power of other positive cards in a reading.

MESSAGE:
Let it flow.

PERSON:
An entrepreneur, a generous man

BODY:
Kidney, bladder, sperm

TIMING:
Full moon, early in the morning

INFLUENCE:
Positive

NUANCE:
Portrait, action

ARCHANGEL:
Raphael

PLANET:
Neptune

ZODIAC SIGN:
Pisces

LOVE (S):
Spontaneous connection, a sense of déjà vu

LOVE (R):
It's all good; the relationship you shared is a great one.

HEALTH:
Vibrant health; stop drinking

MONEY:
Expect money to come to you.

WORK:
Successful ventures, investors

SPECIAL POWER:
The Fish has the power of multiplication: around good cards, it multiplies the positive aspect and around bad cards increases the negative.

35.
THE ANCHOR—9 SPADES

Keyword: Security, Steadiness, Goals

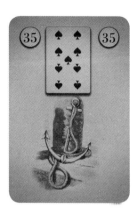

The Anchor denotes that you are being tied securely to a place or a goal. It is also an indication that you are finally reaching a safe harbor and a milestone.

MESSAGE:
You can do it!

BODY:
Pelvis, hips

TIMING:
A long time, years

INFLUENCE:
Positive

NUANCE:
Time

ARCHANGEL:
Michael

PLANET:
Saturn

ZODIAC SIGN:
Capricorn

LOVE (S):
A sincere relationship starts; you have a sense of security about it.

LOVE (R):
The love you share keeps on growing stronger; your destinies are tied together.

HEALTH:
Strong and stable

MONEY:
What you have grows; a secure and stable material situation.

WORK:
Hard work pays off.

SPECIAL POWER:
The Anchor, like a mermaid, has the power to go deep inside of things, both conscious and unconscious.

36.
THE CROSS—6 CLUBS
Keyword: Burden, Troubles

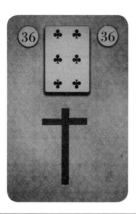

The closer the Cross is to the Significator in a spread, the heavier the burden. The Cross image is associated with the crucifixion; some people see the Cross as the representation of organized and institutional religion. I tend to see the Cross as the card of Karma: what is sent out comes back to you multiplied.

MESSAGE:
Ask for help.

BODY:
Lower back

TIMING:
1 to 6 months

INFLUENCE:
Negative

NUANCE:
Mood

ARCHANGEL:
Michael

PLANET:
Pluto

ZODIAC SIGN:
Libra

LOVE (S):
You are experiencing some hard times.

LOVE (R):
Incomprehension, painful feelings

HEALTH:
Rest more.

MONEY:
Make sacrifices.

WORK:
A difficult time

SPECIAL POWER:
The Cross has the power to make things painful and hard.

ADDITIONAL
KEYWORDS

"THINK LESS. FEEL MORE."
—RUMI

CARD	NUMBER	KEYWORD
Rider	1	News, a delivery or visit. A young, sometimes athletic, person. Speed, agility, and mobility. A horse.
Clover	2	Luck (a little luck), a nice surprise, a new opportunity. Pleasure, enjoyment, happiness, and good fortune. Something green.
Ship	3	Travel, foreigners, and foreign places. Bodies of water. Import/export, trade. Occasionally shows an inheritance.
House	4	Your home in all senses of the word. Real estate. A mature man, often a father or father figure.
Tree	5	Sickness and health. A lengthy amount of time. Boredom, monotony. Growth. Lineage, genealogy, and "roots." Tree, forest, nature.

CARD	NUMBER	KEYWORD
Clouds	6	Problems, haziness, and feeling foggy or clouded. Stormy/cloudy weather, both literal and figuratively. An unpleasant man, sometimes older and very much "in his head." Often, but not always, an ex-husband or ex-boyfriend.
Snake	7	A woman, female rival, or simply a very smart and intellectual lady. Curved shapes, pipes, and tubes. A roundabout, a snake.
Coffin	8	Ending, transformation through finality or completion. Something is dead here. A shock, sickness, loss. Feeling "boxed in." A coffin, a drawer, or a box.
Bouquet	9	An invitation, a welcoming gift/visit/surprise. A pleasant and kind woman. Gift of flowers.
Scythe	10	Suddenness, threat. Possible physical pain as in surgery and cutting. Harvest and gathering. Severing and removing. A young male/Peter Pan complex. A sharp object that can cut. Use with caution.

CARD	NUMBER	KEYWORD
Whip	11	Heated conversations, discussions, or debate. A sharp and tough advisor. Repetitive motion, activity, or rhythm. Repeated addictive behavioral patterns. Passion/obsession, self-sabotage/abuse. (My "sex" card.)
Birds	12	Verbal communication, voice messages, and phone calls. Chatter, anxious talking/ speaking, sometimes gossip or energized dialogue. Things in pairs, siblings, or an older couple.
Child	13	New beginnings, young or new things. Something small in size, a small amount. A child, grandchild. Childlike tendencies.
Fox	14	A false mask, deceit. Someone being wronged. Someone smart. A scam or manipulator. Cunning motives. (My "work" card.)
Bear	15	Executive, boss, or management. Someone of authority in both position and age. Power, force, strength. (My "money" card.)

CARD	NUMBER	KEYWORD
Stars	**16**	Lucidity, psychic development, meeting a clairvoyant. Wishes and wishful thinking. Higher intention and prayer. Things in large number.
Stork	**17**	Changes (usually nice ones), promotion. Upgrade. Moving and relocating, travel. A nice woman, a woman with children or a maternal figure. An "expected" family addition (not always a pregnancy).
Dog	**18**	A good and reliable friend. Someone you can count on. Trust and loyalty. A faithful man. Dog or pet. (My "guardian angel" card.)
Tower	**19**	An official or authority figure. Government and big business. Borders, boundaries, and restrictions. Self-rules, isolation, loneliness, quiet work. A literal tower or tall building.
Garden	**20**	Public places, sites, and locations where people gather: fairs, festivals, events, meetings, parties, entertainment. A park or garden.

CARD	NUMBER	KEYWORD
Mountain	21	Barriers, obstacles, delays. An uphill or circuitous climb. Getting over and above things.
Crossroads	22	Alternatives, choices, decisions. Two ways, direction. A turning point, "being at a crossroad."
Mice	23	Losses, robbery, something that's wearing away or down. Worries, illness, infection, disease. (My card for "stress.")
Heart	24	Love and affection. A warm regard. Sweetheart/friendship, playful flirtation. Feelings of the heart, emotions. Affairs, the "heart's desire." An emotionally mature young man. (My "love" card.)
Ring	25	Contract, pact, partnership. An engagement or long-term commitment. An ongoing loop, series, or sequence. A literal ring. Sometimes a piece of jewelry.

CARD	NUMBER	KEYWORD
Book	26	Secrets, classified information. Academics, higher education, private study. Unrevealed knowledge. Publishing and writing. A literal book.
Letter	27	Written messages/correspondence, information, emails, faxes, memos, notes, missives, receipts, tickets, anything printed out or on paper.
Lilies	30	Tranquility and peace. A strict and mature man or patriarch/protector. Virginity. Winter.
Sun	31	Success! Morning/daylight. Happiness. Heat, fire, warmth, electricity. Brilliance, power, energy, vibrancy. Sunny day. Summer.
Moon	32	Fame and public recognition. Success in creative outlets. Romance. Soul tending. Natural cycles.

CARD	NUMBER	KEYWORD
Key	33	Sureness, complete control, expertise, skill, and talent. A success, a straight "yes" answer. (My "yes" card.)
Fish	34	Money, finances, cash flow, prosperity, and abundance. Deep investment. A sensitive and compassionate businessperson. Liquids, sometimes alcohol. Aquatic life.
Anchor	35	Dropping your anchor. Committing to work, stability, and responsibility. Creating a safe harbor. Retreating to a place of depth.
Cross	36	Suffering, grief, burdens, fate, destiny, challenges, tests, belief, religion. A literal cross.

CARD REVERSALS

"IGNORANCE IS GOD'S PRISON.
KNOWING IS GOD'S PALACE."
—RUMI

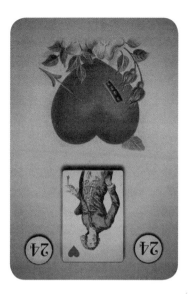 

From the French perspective of Lenormand, the cards are never read reversed. Even if they happen to appear as so, the reader would simply flip the card in the upright position. When it comes to learning the system, the 36 cards have enough information and stories to tell—you don't need another layer of 36 that would come with adding reversals. Imagine how overwhelming and confusing it might be when you would have to deal The Grand Tableau and its Houses.

In Tarot, reversals work wonderfully, but not in Lenormand; the two systems are distinctive, and I prefer to keep them separate. One can successfully use Tarot in conjunction with Lenormand, though, if you keep in mind that with Lenormand, wherever the Heart 24 is blue or black, pierced with swords and arrows, it will always mean romance and feelings of love. Whereas with the Tarot, the meaning takes on another direction, which would be more of a broken heart, a deception, or a wounded heart. This is a common mistake that Tarot readers make; they tend to "Tarotize" Lenormand, and this drives them to confusion and discouragement with their readings. I started with playing cards, continued with Lenormand, and then studied the Tarot; I must admit that my apprenticeship was a bit easier, as I had no other systems to influence my Lenormand readings, and I could keep them separate. Once you understand the unique voice of Lenormand, and allow yourself to experience the system, the voice becomes stronger and more distinctive, and the magic can occur.

LENORMAND
SIGNIFICATORS

"DO YOU KNOW WHAT YOU ARE?
YOU ARE A MANUSCRIPT OF A DIVINE LETTER."
—RUMI

A "Significator," also known as "key card," "charge card," or "activated card," is a card that holds the meaning or focus of the central topic, or querent, for the reading. The Man 28 represents the male querent and the Woman 29 represents the female querent; this never changes. You can also preselect a particular card in the deck for the topic of your reading. For instance, in a love question, you may use the Heart 24; for a family-related question, use the House 4; for a business transaction you will use the Fish 34. A Significator can have more than one meaning, depending on the context of your question.

In the following chart, you will find examples of cards that can be used as Significators for different types of questions.

NUMBER	CARD	SIGNIFICATOR
1	Rider	Male third party
3	Ship	Travel
4	House	Family, property
5	Tree	Health
7	Snake	Female third party
13	Child	Pregnancy, child-raising, a kid
14	Fox	Work
15	Bear	Money
17	Stork	Pregnancy, moving to a new house
18	Dog	Partner, friendship, pet

NUMBER	CARD	SIGNIFICATOR
19	Tower	Court case
20	Garden	Parties, meetings, festivities
24	Heart	Love and romance
25	Ring	Marriage, union, partnership
26	Book	Education, deals
27	Letter	Document, messages
28	Man	The male querent
29	Woman	The female querent
34	Fish	Transaction, purchase, sales
35	Anchor	Goal and target

HOW TO USE THE SIGNIFICATOR TO REPLY TO A QUESTION

Frame your question and choose a Significator from the chart that best fits your question. Focus on the question and the Significator as you shuffle your deck. Then, go through the deck until you find the Significator you've chosen and take out all the cards that sandwich the Significator—that is, the cards before and after it. Here is an example:

Marie wants to know if the letter she is waiting for is lost. I will use here The Letter 27 as the Significator to represent the letter Marie is expecting. I shuffle and run through the deck looking for the Letter 27 card; I take the cards before and after it and I get:

MICE 23—LETTER 27—MOUNTAIN 21

My interpretation:
The letter is lost or blocked somewhere; I am not seeing it reaching Marie.

(Mice 23 meaning loss; Mountain 21 meaning delays or obstacles.)

This is a simple and quick method that can help you clearly answer a question. In the following example, I will show how a Significator can have varied meanings for different areas of one's life.

JOB CARDS

There are four cards that represent work and career in the Lenormand deck: Fox 14, Bear 15, Tower 19, and Anchor 35. Depending on the tradition or school that you use, one of these four cards would be the Significator you would use for a work question. In my system, I use them all together to provide greater depth in a reading; let me show you how:

The Fox is my job card in general; it symbolizes your day job, what brings food to the table, what pays the bills and takes care of the family. It can also be a part-time job.

The Bear stands for the boss. If you are an executive or a CEO, the Bear would represent you or any person having this type of position.

The Tower stands for a corporation, the headquarters, and a structured organization or institution; things get more disciplined with the Tower.

The Anchor is a stable job, something for long-term; a full-time job, a well-established career. I see the Anchor as a job requiring hard work, not necessarily physically but something that engages your best skills in some way.

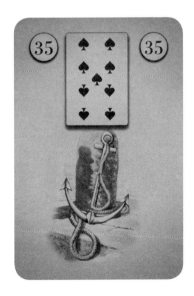

LOVE AND RELATIONSHIPS

The Heart 24 and the Ring 25 are the main cards that represent relationships in a romantic perspective. With love being the number one question that clients ask about during a reading, you must know when to use the Ring and when to use the Heart.

The Heart is about love and affection, having warm regard. Being one of the mood cards, it describes the feelings for someone: Does he love me? Will she forgive me?

The Ring stands for a contract, pact, partnership, engagement, and long-term commitment. Being a portrait card, the Ring describes the intentions of someone: Will he propose to me? Will I sign the contract?

HEALTH CARDS

I use three cards that directly speak about health in Lenormand: Tree 5, Tower 19, and Scythe 10.

The Tree stands for general health. In a Grand Tableau, the closer the Tree is to the Significator card (28 or 29), the more health issues will be the focus. An exception is when cards having trees in them are nearby (for instance the Garden 20); this would predict vibrant health.

The Tower stands for longevity; in a health reading, its proximity to the querent cards (28 and 29) assures strong health and a long life.

The Scythe is a cutting instrument with a sharp blade. In a health reading, the Scythe indicates that the querent may have surgery.

MONEY CARDS

The three cards that I use for money are: the Clover 2, Bear 15, and the Fish 34. Each card talks about money, but relates differently to amount earned, gained, or spent.

For example, money represented by the Clover is unexpected, won most often via gambling. The amount is small, not as substantial as winning the lottery and becoming a millionaire!

In traditional French cartomancy, the Ten of Clubs represents money, and I think that early French Lenormand readers applied this meaning of great abundance to the Bear. The amount of money is bigger than that of the Clover (the source for Bear would surely come from work—a salary).

The Fish is a card of abundance and prosperity; whatever is near the Fish gets multiplied. My favorite keyword for the Fish is "Plenty"; it increases your revenue and, with good combinations, the Fish alludes to wealth to the point of being a millionaire.

"A WEALTH YOU CANNOT IMAGINE
FLOWS THROUGH YOU."
—RUMI

THE LANGUAGE OF LENORMAND

"AS YOU START TO WALK OUT ON THE WAY,
THE WAY APPEARS."
—RUMI

Now that you've mastered the card meanings, it is time to explain how Lenormand cards are read. The cards use a language of their own. Again, most important, do not read them like you would read the Tarot. Lenormand symbols mean the same whatever deck you are using. What I mean is that the Rider will always mean news or an unexpected visit, even when depicted with one riding a camel or a giraffe. Remember when you were in kindergarten, the teacher would use flashcards to teach a word associated with a picture? When seeing the apple card, you would say "apple" despite its color. The Fox is always cunning even if it is depicted as a white fox in a snowy décor or brown in another scene. Likewise, the Key will always announce success, no matter whether it is made of gold, silver, or metal. Think of reading the Lenormand as reading a pictogram or hieroglyph of universal symbols.

Let's look at how to understand the language of the Lenormand. The cards are never read individually; they are read as a fusion of one card with another to create a sentence or a message. Begin your associations by assigning at least two keywords to each individual card, choosing the one that best fits the reader's context. For instance, Bouquet = gifts, proposition; and Ring = commitment, deal.

With a question in mind, shuffle your cards and pull two cards, combining the keywords of each card together. Keep in mind the context of your question. What I mean here by "context" is that card meanings will not be the same for this combination of cards regarding a love question versus one regarding a job opportunity. Let me use an example so you can clearly see what I am talking about.

Mary wants to know: Will I get married to John this year?
The cards I pulled are the Stork 17 and the House 4. The cards show that there is some kind of move going on, a change—not a separation, as the house suggests comfort, intimacy, and being between four walls. The cards are clearly telling about a move-in situation.

My answer to Mary:
There is no marriage for you this year, but John will start by asking you to move in with him.

Let's practice some more.
John wants to know: Will I get the job promotion?

His cards are the Stork 17 and the Ring 25. The first thing many think is that the Ring means only marriage, and the Stork pregnancy, but the meanings can vary depending on context. This is important to pay attention to if you want your readings to be accurate. This combo tells us that John will definitely get his job promotion, as the Stork and Ring foretell of an agreement for a step up, or positive change.

Like learning a foreign language via Lenormand symbols, your brain needs to learn to assimilate symbols and concepts via vocabulary, modifiers, and phrasing. My high school English teacher used to say, "Practice makes perfect." Practice as much as possible; train yourself by making predictions on various topics such as: everyday issues, national decisions, the election, or the sex of your neighbors forthcoming child.

Work your gift as much as you can!

The next chapter provides a useful tool: an extensive list of Lenormand combinations for each of the 36 cards. Refer to it in your readings as needed. But this list is by no means exhaustive; I invite you to play, create, and add your own. Keep a special notebook for this purpose where you can chart your own combined meanings and refer to it as often as needed.

Some examples of combinations:

Child + Dog, we get:
- ❖ A new friendship
- ❖ A young friend
- ❖ A small dog, or pet

Coffin + Scythe
- ❖ The end of a difficult situation
- ❖ A separation
- ❖ An accident

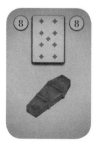
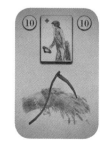

LENORMAND CARD
COMBINATIONS

 +  =

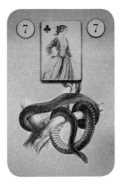 +  = ?

This chapter lists combinations for each of the 36 Lenormand cards. It will be a handy reference for learning about and understanding card combinations. Choose the meaning that best suits the context of your question for the cards you choose and link their meanings. It can happen that during a reading you feel stuck with a combination; the list becomes handy to help you continue forward with your reading. You can also look at the two different combos, A+B and B+A. Be creative and remember to play. Note that not all combos listed here will be applicable. With time and experience, you will gradually build your own combined meanings. Until then, let this resource help you get started.

1. RIDER

2. Clover: Unexpected event, lucky strike, good news, a positive change

3. Ship: News from a foreign country, someone coming from far

4. House: Unexpected visitor, a message about property

5. Tree: Health-related information, a past-life issue

6. Clouds: Bad or confusing information, troubling news

7. Snake: False message, news from a woman. Pay attention!

8. Coffin: An ending, news of someone passing, a depressed man

9. Bouquet: A proposal, someone bringing a gift, a surprise

10. Scythe: Surgery, breaking a leg, an accident

11. Whip: An argument, an athletic or sexy man

12. Birds: An interview, verbal news, two boys/men

13. Child: Birth announcement, a new start, a young boy

14. Fox: False message, work-related information

15. Bear: Information related to finances, a message from a boss

16. Stars: Famous man, inspiring message, many messages

17. Stork: Birth announcement, a change for the better

18. Dog: A faithful friend, message from a friend, a new friend

19. Tower: Official news, news from the government, a lonely man

20. Garden: Public announcement, news from social media or networks

21. Mountain: A cancelled visit, delayed message, a postponement

22. Crossroads: Indecisive man, news about a decision, a verdict

23. Mice: Stressful news, lost information

24. Heart: Messages from a loved one, a message of love, a new love

25. Ring: Wedding announcement, news about a deal or contract

26. Book: Secret messages, secret relationship, a discovery

27. Letter: Written messages, documents, the postman

28. Man: A new man, news for the querent, unexpected visit

29. Woman: Another man, a lover, news for the querent

30. Lilies: News from an elder, long awaited information

31. Sun: Good news, joyous man, an achievement

32. Moon: Emotive information, news about one's reputation

33. Key: News of success, a solution comes forward, a helpful man

34. Fish: News about finances, work and business ventures, a foreigner

35. Anchor: A confirmed piece of information, a strong man

36. Cross: News of trouble, stressful information

2. CLOVER

1. Rider: Lucky man, hazel eyes, Irish man, a gambler

3. Ship: Lucky trip, change of luck, a positive change

4. House: Prosperous house, lucky acquisition

5. Tree: Green diet, recovering from an illness

6. Clouds: Laziness, misfortune, bad luck, a blockage

7. Snake: Woman with hazel eyes, a gambler, lucky woman

8. Coffin: Risky situation, end of luck, bad luck

9. Bouquet: Great luck, lucky opportunities, positive situation

10. Scythe: Lucky decision, give it a chance, sudden luck

11. Whip: Repetitive lucky situations, a winner, winning a medal

12. Birds: Positive affirmations, a lucky conversation

13. Child: Small luck, beginner's luck, fresh start on a positive note

14. Fox: Professional gambler, forcing your luck, job opportunity

15. Bear: Lucky gambler, big luck, a lucky boss

16. Stars: Many opportunities, good luck, divine synchronicities

17. Stork: A positive change, moving to a green area, improvement

18. Dog: A lucky friend, a positive friend, a lucky relationship

19. Tower: Casino or gambling place, video games, arcades

20. Garden: Games, board games, team game, winning team

21. Mountain: Blockage, standstill, misfortune

22. Crossroads: Lucky decision, multiple choices, countryside

23. Mice: Bad luck, money loss, a warning to be prudent

24. Heart: Lucky in love, heart chakra, feeling lucky

25. Ring: Lucky deal, lucky contract, lucky union

26. Book: Discovery, cookbook, unknown luck, unknown fortune

27. Letter: Positive news, lottery ticket, news of a gain

28. Man/29. Woman: Lucky man, hazel eyes, positive person

30. Lilies: Success at last, a lucky situation

31. Sun: Big luck, overnight success

32. Moon: Good reputation, a sudden inspiration

33. Key: A lot of success, lucky solution, a powerful talisman

34. Fish: Financial abundance, good transaction, lucky with money

35. Anchor: Long-term prosperity, reaching a significant milestone

36. Cross: Positive ending, blessing in disguise

3. SHIP

1. Rider: Lucky man, hazel eyes, Irish man

2. Clover: Unexpected trip, successful trip

4. House: Traveling to your native land, boathouse

5. Tree: Sea sickness, traveling for health, long journey

6. Clouds: Uncertain trip, confusing trip, delayed trip

7. Snake: A detour, traveling with a woman

8. Coffin: Cancellation, a parcel

9. Bouquet: Gift from abroad, unexpected trip

10. Scythe: Cancelled journey, an accident

11. Whip: Active exhausting journey, repetitive trip

12. Birds: Talking about a trip or vacation, international call

13. Child: Starting a journey, young foreigner, a small trip

14. Fox: Business trip, working in the traveling agency

15. Bear: Traveling with your boss, money from abroad, inheritance

16. Stars: Various trips, dreamed vacation, a cruise under the stars

17. Stork: Moving house, leaving for a foreign country

18. Dog: Foreign friends, traveling with a friend

19. Tower: Traveling alone, government-related travel

20. Garden: Tour operator, traveling in a group, traveling to a gathering

21. Mountain: A blocked trip, a breakdown, delayed flight

22. Crossroads: Transit, two itineraries, deciding about a trip

23. Mice: Stressful trip, losing direction, getting lost

24. Heart: Honeymoon, a romantic trip, a desired trip

25. Ring: Wedding trip, traveling for a deal or contract

26. Book: Secret travel, educational trip, a passport

27. Letter: A visa, flight ticket, information about a trip

28. Man: Foreigner, getting an inheritance, a sailor, a marine

29. Woman: Foreigner, getting an inheritance

30. Lilies: Traveling to a snowy place, travel with or to an elder

31. Sun: A great trip, a vacation, traveling during the day

32. Moon: A romantic trip, traveling by night, an intuitive trip

33. Key: A successful and protected trip, a good business venture

34. Fish: A good investment, traveling for business, income

35. Anchor: Reaching your destination, boats, a cruise

36. Cross: Painful trip, a difficult transition, a pilgrimage

4. HOUSE

1. Rider: Unexpected visitors, news about your house or a property

2. Clover: A good home, a positive possession

3. Ship: Changing residence, living on a boat

5. Tree: A nursing home, a place that feels good

6. Clouds: Problems at home, confused family

7. Snake: A trap, problems at home, an enemy in the family

8. Coffin: Family death, an empty house, an abandoned property

9. Bouquet: Happy house, a surprise party, beautiful house

10. Scythe: House renovation, selling a house, letting go of a property

11. Whip: Domestic violence, arguments at home, heated conversation

12. Birds: Co-location, gossip at home, a noisy house

13. Child: A small house, a new house, a cottage

14. Fox: Domestic employee, home-office, a latent defect, housekeeper

15. Bear: A big house, buying a house, investing in real estate

16. Stars: Many houses, a dreamed home, a city

17. Stork: Moving, relocation, a better house

18. Dog: A friendly home, a protected house, a friendly atmosphere

19. Tower: Flat, residence, apartments, isolated house

20. Garden: Hotel, family reunion, a villa

21. Mountain: A blockage in an acquisition, house on the highlands

22. Crossroads: A decision regarding a property, two houses

23. Mice: Stressful family issues, losing a house, house in ruin

24. Heart: Loving house, loving family, a loving atmosphere

25. Ring: Real estate contract, house or rent deal

26. Book: Unknown house, house of secret, secret life

27. Letter: House contract, property title, house plan

28. Man: House owner, landlord, man at home

29. Woman: House owner, landlord, housewife

30. Lilies: Old house, ancient property, family harmony

31. Sun: Successful family, bright house, good energy

32. Moon: Dreamed house, calm and serene house

33. Key: The house is yours, ownership, the solution

34. Fish: Real estate transaction, purchasing a house, investing

35. Anchor: Committed family, long-term acquisition

36. Cross: Past life with a house or place, heavy atmosphere

5. TREE

1. Rider: Health-related news, visiting a sick person

2. Clover: Recovering from illness, plants, crops

3. Ship: Car repair, traveling to see a sick person

4. House: Native home, a tree house, healthy family, family tree

6. Clouds: Health issue, mental confusion, hallucination

7. Snake: Female doctor, virus, infection

8. Coffin: Severe depression, health issues, dead tree

9. Bouquet: Good health, health improvement, healthy proposition

10. Scythe: Surgery, broken bones, an incision

11. Whip: Muscular pain, muscle disease, poor health

12. Birds: Therapy, healthy conversation, good discussion

13. Child: Childhood illness, small disease, pregnancy

14. Fox: Misdiagnosis, health caretaker, a gardener

15. Bear: Eating disorder, obesity, difficulty losing weight

16. Stars: Healing, recovery, expansion of disease

17. Stork: Pregnancy, birth, recovery

18. Dog: Good friend, soulmate, strong connection

19. Tower: Hospital, depression, clinic

20. Garden: Spa, garden, healthy and balanced relationship

21. Mountain: Fatigue, illness, blockage

22. Crossroads: Second opinion, spiritual path, health decision

23. Mice: Anxiety, stress, illness

24. Heart: Heart problems, healthy heart, heart connection

25. Ring: Past-life connection, pattern, repeated issue

26. Book: Unknown health issue, checkup, health record

27. Letter: Prescription, lab results, health certificate

28. Man/29. Woman: Sick man, healer, a doctor

30. Lilies: Age-related illness, old tree

31. Sun: Sunburn, dehydration, vitamin D deficiency

32. Moon: Hormone disorder, menopause, depression

33. Key: Recovery, perfect health, significant improvement

34. Fish: An increase in your income, prosperity, medical expenses

35. Anchor: Stable health, your health is safe

36. Cross: Depression, tension, pain

6. CLOUDS

1. Rider: Confusing messages, bad news, slow progression

2. Clover: Bad luck, trouble of all sorts, blockage, misfortune

3. Ship: Dangerous journey, confusing change, uncertain travel

4. House: Family trouble, disappointment, uncomfortable home

5. Tree: Stress and depression, sickness, mental illness

7. Snake: Danger, complicated woman, drama queen, lies

8. Coffin: Depression, suicidal thoughts, confinement

9. Bouquet: Sadness, bad surprise, unpleasant gift

10. Scythe: Complicated and unsure surgery, end of confusion

11. Whip: Argument, pattern and bad behavior, violence

12. Birds: Confusing conversation, gossip, lies

13. Child: Disappointment right at the start, confused child

14. Fox: Liar, manipulation, avid smoker, dealer

15. Bear: Big confusion, trouble with a boss, trouble with your mother

16. Stars: Feeling lost and uncertain, drug abuse, loss of fame

17. Stork: Dangerous move, unpleasant woman

18. Dog: Dishonest friend, false friend, confused friendship

19. Tower: Confused judgment, self-sabotage, unsettled

20. Garden: Emotional tension, confusing relationship, uncertain connection

21. Mountain: A failure, delays, danger, nothing good

22. Crossroads: Doubts, uncertainty, indecision, fear

23. Mice: Stressful situation, small doubts

24. Heart: Uncertain about your true feelings, incomprehension

25. Ring: Confuse alliance, uncertain contract, stalemate situation

26. Book: Secrets, unknown fact keeps you upset

27. Letter: Bad news, confusing news, sad news

28. Man/29. Woman: Anxious, preoccupied, confused man

30. Lilies: Anxious, grumpy man, dishonest person

31. Sun: Things are getting better, sunlight after the storm

32. Moon: Mood swings, depression, obsession, preoccupation

33. Key: Solution found in time, delayed success

34. Fish: Debt, uncertainty about finances, confused transaction

35. Anchor: Deep disorder, patience is needed to overcome the problem

36. Cross: Anxiety, grief, sadness, tears

7. SNAKE

1. Rider: A troubled relationship, news of a betrayal, message from a rival

2. Clover: Some may be jealous of your luck

3. Ship: Troubled trip, traveling with a woman

4. House: Betrayal, lies, a jealous family member

5. Tree: Jealousy and envy firmly rooted, be cautious, danger

6. Clouds: Confusion, a trap

8. Coffin: End of problems, ending for a woman (unclear)

9. Bouquet: Beautiful, charming, dangerous woman, two women

10. Scythe: Putting an end to murky relationship, surgery for a woman

11. Whip: Conflict, aggression, violence

12. Birds: Insults, gossip, discussion with a woman

13. Child: Spoiled child, new danger

14. Fox: Trouble at work, female rival, manipulation

15. Bear: Mother-in-law, a female boss, a toxic boss

16. Stars: Many dangers, jealous of your popularity, famous woman

17. Stork: Change that involves danger, two women

18. Dog: Dangerous friendship, toxic female friend, jealousy from friends

19. Tower: Lawsuit, injustice, using unconventional ways

20. Garden: Disappointment and sadness from the hypocrisy of friends

21. Mountain: A dangerous enemy

22. Crossroads: A difficult choice. Run from this woman!

23. Mice: Stressful woman, a woman loses something

24. Heart: A rival, dangerous feeling

25. Ring: False commitment, compromise

26. Book: Secret enemy, secret woman, dangerous secret

27. Letter: Bad news, more lies, threat letter

28. Man: Another woman, a rival, a false man

29. Woman: Woman with a girlfriend, a cheater

30. Lilies: Lack of confidence, disloyal person

31. Sun: A successfully woman, an enemy is defeated

32. Moon: Bad reputation, popular woman, disillusion

33. Key: The manipulative woman succeeds in her plan

34. Fish: Receiving money through unconventional ways

35. Anchor: Insecurity, a stable woman

36. Cross: An abuse, harmful situation

8. COFFIN

1. Rider: News of someone passing, messages from above, rebirth

2. Clover: A second chance, end of misfortune

3. Ship: A change, a transformation

4. House: Illness or death of a family member

5. Tree: Illness, dangerous health issue

6. Clouds: Mental illness, depression

7. Snake: Dangerous enemy, negative influences

9. Bouquet: End of a stressful time, happiness returns

10. Scythe: Accident, surgery

11. Whip: Violence, threat

12. Birds: End of conversation, sad confidence

13. Child: Sick child, destructive child

14. Fox: Losing your job, retirement

15. Bear: Receiving a donation, strong confinement

16. Stars: Positive transformation, serenity

17. Stork: Moving house, a big change

18. Dog: Sick friend, friend in grief

19. Tower: Confinement, isolation, jail

20. Garden: Cemetery, a postponed event, a cancellation

21. Mountain: Isolation, stuck point, handicap

22. Crossroads: New horizon, new direction

23. Mice: Something that eats away at you, stress

24. Heart: Heartache, grief, deception

25. Ring: A relationship ending, cancelling a contract, a completion

26. Book: A secret is revealed

27. Letter: Negative message, news about someone passing

28. Man: Negative man, sick man

29. Woman: Negative woman, sick woman

30. Lilies: Death, something ends here

31. Sun: Success at last, happy ending

32. Moon: Grief, painful feelings, mentally tired

33. Key: The end of a period of misfortune, a solution is found

34. Fish: Retirement, out of business, end of transaction

35. Anchor: Incurable disease, end of stability

36. Cross: Pain, sadness, grief, nostalgia

9. BOUQUET

1. Rider: Good surprise, happy news, handsome man
2. Clover: Good luck, positive outcome
3. Ship: Beautiful trip, beautiful car, positive change
4. House: Lovely home, gifted family, beautiful family
5. Tree: Good health, healing
6. Clouds: Daydreaming, wishful thinking, laziness
7. Snake: Two women, jealousy, envy, a fashionista
8. Coffin: Disappointment, unpleasant surprise
10. Scythe: Positive surgery, a happy conclusion
11. Whip: Unpleasant situation that ruins the day
12. Birds: Positive talk, nice conversation, talking about fashion
13. Child: Beautiful child, *joie de vivre*, happiness
14. Fox: Happiness at work, the fashion industry, work proposal
15. Bear: Your finances are good, happy mother, happy boss
16. Stars: Achievement, reaching a milestone, happiness
17. Stork: Positive change, happiness is on its way
18. Dog: Positive friendship, a happy friend, a beautiful friendship
19. Tower: Pleasant memories, being in good company
20. Garden: A get-together, pleasant social gatherings, a picnic
21. Mountain: A positive attitude when faced with challenges, blessing in disguise
22. Crossroads: A change for the better, new opportunities
23. Mice: Short happiness, paying a debt, returning a borrowed object
24. Heart: Renewal of feeling, true love, positive relationship
25. Ring: A wedding proposal, happy marriage, a contract
26. Book: Reading or writing for enjoyment, a self-help book
27. Letter: News that makes you happy, good news
28. Man: A positive man, generous, pleasant, a real gentleman
29. Woman: A positive woman, generous, pleasant, a beautiful woman
30. Lilies: Peacefulness, serenity, calmness
31. Sun: Bright and beautiful future, success in all areas of life
32. Moon: Satisfaction, a romantic date, a positive rendezvous
33. Key: Unexpected success, everything finally turns out in a great way
34. Fish: Purchasing something that makes you happy, good investment
35. Anchor: Deep down feelings of happiness, stability, and security
36. Cross: You are destined to be happy and to make others happy

10. SCYTHE

1. Rider: Sudden message, an ending that enables other things to emerge

2. Clover: A positive change, a strike of luck

3. Ship: Taking distance, a trip canceled, a brutal change

4. House: A sudden change, a change in residence

5. Tree: Surgery, an illness, an injury

6. Clouds: Indecision, brutal change, an upsetting situation

7. Snake: A danger, your life may be in danger, dangerous enemy

8. Coffin: An ending, a transformation, a rebirth

9. Bouquet: Positive change, positive outcome, a change for the better

11. Whip: A sudden argument, an argument you didn't see coming

12. Birds: Not caring what people say, ending a speculation

13. Child: Something new, new idea, new inspiration

14. Fox: Job loss, walking away from a situation, agricultural worker

15. Bear: Financial decision, a surgery for weight loss, fast food

16. Stars: Changing your mind, taking action toward your dreams

17. Stork: A fast change, a fast move, a C-section

18. Dog: Cutting a friend off, ending a friendship, pet getting a surgery

19. Tower: Letting go of the past, end of anarchy, being free, liberation

20. Garden: A cancelled gathering, being in dangerous company

21. Mountain: Cutting through obstacles, breaking things into small pieces

22. Crossroads: Sudden decision, a sudden change, quick decision

23. Mice: The end of an annoying situation, end of worries

24. Heart: Heartbreak, a separation, the end of a relationship

25. Ring: Divorce, end of a partnership, a separation, cutting ties

26. Book: Learning something unexpected, discovering a secret

27. Letter: Bad news, unexpected news, a threat letter

28. Man: Decisive man, ending something, making a radical decision

29. Woman: Decisive woman, ending something, making a radical decision

30. Lilies: Loss of virginity, sexual aggression, a rape

31. Sun: A change for the better, unexpected good fortune

32. Moon: Emotional decision, putting an end to wishful thinking

33. Key: A breakthrough, sudden success

34. Fish: A cut in income, unexpected changes in your income

35. Anchor: Breaking free of something that had tied you down

36. Cross: A major change in your belief system

11. WHIP

1. Rider: News of an argument, unpleasant visit

2. Clover: Lucky action, forcing your luck, a champion

3. Ship: Another trip, troubled and hard journey

4. House: Family arguments, family violence

5. Tree: Painful health issues, repetitive illness, sexual disease

6. Clouds: Confusing argument, a pattern, repetitive trouble

7. Snake: Danger, a troublemaker, a woman claiming vengeance

8. Coffin: Destruction, physical abuse, ending an argument

9. Bouquet: Dancing, Zumba®, fun physical activity

10. Scythe: Accident, danger, violence

12. Birds: People talking behind your back, being the subject of an argument

13. Child: A new argument, argument with a child, small argument

14. Fox: Athlete, working hard, argument at work

15. Bear: An official argument, a court case, an abusive mother

16. Stars: Many arguments, successful competition, coaching

17. Stork: Resolving an old argument, moving past the argument

18. Dog: A violent friend, disagreement with a friend or partner

19. Tower: Sports industry, trouble with the authorities, a court case

20. Garden: Public debates, public sporting event, public violence

21. Mountain: Argument that leads nowhere, not finding a solution

22. Crossroads: Difficult choice, forced to choose, wrong decision

23. Mice: Hurtful comments, exhaustion, moral harassment

24. Heart: Wounded heart, emotional conflict, hate

25. Ring: Abuse, a difficult marriage, troubled relationship

26. Book: Hidden trouble, academic competition, an examination or test

27. Letter: Bad news, threat, unpleasant words

28. Man/29. Woman: Intense, physical person

30. Lilies: Tired, exhausted, a rude man attacks a gentleman

31. Sun: An argument with a good outcome, sorting out problems

32. Moon: A troublesome invitation or conversation, an illusion

33. Key: Overcoming drama, success after struggle

34. Fish: Financial difficulty, needing to "borrow from Peter to pay Paul"

35. Anchor: Disagreement that doesn't find any solution, waste of time

36. Cross: A hard lesson, repetitive hard situation

12. BIRDS

1. Rider: Announcing the visit of two persons, good news

2. Clover: Lucky conversation that brings in new opportunities

3. Ship: Talking about a trip or a change, migrating to a foreign country

4. House: Real estate discussions, talking with a relative

5. Tree: Throat issue, spiritual discussions, health discussions

6. Clouds: Confusing conversation, misunderstanding

7. Snake: Gossip, conversing with a dangerous woman, prudence

8. Coffin: End of a conversation, silence, not replying back

9. Bouquet: Happy conversation, talking about opportunities

10. Scythe: Difficult negotiation, interrupting a conversation

11. Whip: Talking about the same thing again and again, argument

13. Child: Rumors about a child, new conversation, twins

14. Fox: Rumors and gossip, job related conversation, lies, flattery

15. Bear: Talking with the boss, big conversation, important exchange

16. Stars: Many conversations, spreading gossip

17. Stork: Rumors about a pregnancy, new topic, international phone call

18. Dog: Conversing with friends, friend who likes rumors and gossip

19. Tower: Legal discussions, talking about the past, old talks

20. Garden: Gossiping about an event, a meeting, a conference

21. Mountain: Discussing a problem, making plans

22. Crossroads: Talking about the future, phone call concerning a decision

23. Mice: Stressful talks, discussing a debt, suspicion of a robbery

24. Heart: Heartfelt conversation, the lovers, lovely couple

25. Ring: Rumors about a divorce, an agreement, marriage counseling

26. Book: Secret conversation, learning to talk, unknown rumors

27. Letter: Vocal message, the media, paparazzi, interview

28. Man/29. Woman: Talkative, a good speaker, a mediator, a counselor

30. Lilies: Trustworthy conversation, a very long discussion

31. Sun: Successful interview, a bright conversation, nice exchange

32. Moon: Creative and productive conversation, talking about your desires

33. Key: A conversation that brings a solution, an answer to a question

34. Fish: Financial talks, talking about expenditures and budget

35. Anchor: Deep conversation, a persistent rumor

36. Cross: A prayer, asking for help, heavy words

13. CHILD

1. Rider: New visit, fresh start, small move
2. Clover: Small luck, new opportunity, positive start
3. Ship: New travel, new movement, small trip
4. House: Small house, new house, new family, babysitting
5. Tree: Sick child, fertility issues, child raising
6. Clouds: Confused child, blocked child
7. Snake: Jealous child, dangerous child, small danger, new danger
8. Coffin: New beginning, new transition, an abortion, a miscarriage
9. Bouquet: Beautiful and pleasant child, small gift, new happiness
10. Scythe: Abortion, surgery, sick child, childhood illness
11. Whip: Bullied child, abused child, small argument
12. Birds: Short conversation, new conversation
14. Fox: First job, new job, part-time job
15. Bear: A protected child, a vigorous and strong child with a large appetite
16. Stars: Lucky child, gifted child, remarkable child
17. Stork: A pregnancy, an adoption, new beginning, a new residence
18. Dog: Childhood friend, new friendship, child with a pet
19. Tower: Childhood, school, small building
20. Garden: Kindergarten, playground, classroom
21. Mountain: Small obstacle, a new challenge
22. Crossroads: A new direction, a new path
23. Mice: Small payment, a refund, small loss, a sick child
24. Heart: A generous person, new love, a young lover
25. Ring: New alliance, new contract, son/daughter in-law
26. Book: Small secret, homework, schooling, apprenticeship
27. Letter: Birth announcement, happy news
28. Man: Naïve, childish, immature, man with children
29. Woman: Naïve, childish, immature, woman with children
30. Lilies: Older child, loyal and honest child
31. Sun: Happy child, healed child, playful child
32. Moon: Small acknowledgment, creative child, new moon
33. Key: Successful and clever child, successful new start
34. Fish: Small income, new business, small business
35. Anchor: Working with children, strong child
36. Cross: Painful childhood, sad child, sad start

14. FOX

1. Rider: News about a job, a tricky message or visit

2. Clover: Lucky job, taking a chance on this job

3. Ship: Traveling for work, working in foreign countries

4. House: Home office, a red house, a false family member

5. Tree: A doctor, a healer, a misdiagnosis

6. Clouds: Dishonest worker, confusing job or task

7. Snake: A liar, dangerous and risky job, manipulation

8. Coffin: Leaving a job, completing a job

9. Bouquet: Charming, redhead woman, a seductive woman

10. Scythe: Work accident, finishing a job

11. Whip: A policeman, a detective, sex worker

12. Birds: Cunning conversation, tricky conversation

13. Child: First job, new job, part-time job

15. Bear: Well-paid job, being your own boss

16. Stars: Serenity, a job promotion, a recognition

17. Stork: Job change, a bizarre change, suspicious change

18. Dog: Cunning friend, false friendship, manipulative friend

19. Tower: Police station, beauty industry, a lawyer

20. Garden: Fox in the henhouse, escaping your responsibilities

21. Mountain: Unable to see a way through, worries related to work

22. Crossroads: Multiple jobs, unwise choice, two-job option, a copycat

23. Mice: Stressful job, losing a job, coveting someone else's position

24. Heart: Loving your job, untrustworthy love, doubtful feeling

25. Ring: Work contract, false agreement, arranged marriage

26. Book: Investigation, conspiracy, cheating on an exam

27. Letter: Suspicious document, read between the lines, false document

28. Man/29. Woman: Cunning, smart, cheater, redhead, clever, undercover

30. Lilies: Peaceful at work, older employee, established job

31. Sun: Successful work, lies are discovered, truth wins

32. Moon: Psychic, intuitive, undercover, magician

33. Key: Meaningful job, work-related solution, job answer

34. Fish: Financial fraud, counterfeit money

35. Anchor: Long-term job, fraud going on for a long time

36. Cross: Lying for a long time, lies bringing suffering

15. BEAR

1. Rider: Your mother visits you, financial news, important news

2. Clover: Great luck, prosperity, advancement

3. Ship: Money transfer, inheritance, long travel

4. House: Big house, family house, property

5. Tree: Diet, eating disorders, health care

6. Clouds: Uncertain financial situation, poor investment

7. Snake: Dangerous investor, big jealousy, financial issue

8. Coffin: Bankruptcy, financial loss, sick mother

9. Bouquet: Prosperous situation, a good boss, a beautiful mother

10. Scythe: Closing an account, ending an investment

11. Whip: Violence, fighting for money

12. Birds: Financial conversation, talking to your mother

13. Child: New investment, things can start small and then grow big

14. Fox: Dishonest boss, cunning boss, financial problem

16. Stars: Famous boss, financial achievement, good investment

17. Stork: New boss, financial change, financial improvement

18. Dog: Friendly boss, friends in high positions, trustworthy investment

19. Tower: Courthouse, bank, corporation

20. Garden: Big gathering, work team, a large company

21. Mountain: Financial blocks, investment of paramount importance

22. Crossroads: Multiple sources of income, financial decision

23. Mice: Paying a fee, financial stress, a worried mother

24. Heart: Loving mother, a generous boss, strong feelings

25. Ring: Financial deal, transaction, big wedding, important date

26. Book: Secret investment, big secret, strong knowledge

27. Letter: An official letter, a check, an invoice, a contract

28. Man/ 29. Woman: Person with extra pounds, manager, someone with a big appetite

30. Lilies: Steady financial situation, long-term prosperity

31. Sun: Successful investment, big success, prosperous situation

32. Moon: Royalties, dividend, commissions

33. Key: Important financial success, successful investment

34. Fish: Seafood, an amazing sum of money, a big purchase

35. Anchor: Secure financial situation, hard work pays off

36. Cross: Heavy responsibility, financial burden

16. STARS

1. Rider: Good news, news spreading quickly, big news

2. Clover: Lucky strike, make a wish, good luck

3. Ship: Overseas travel, many journeys, dreamed trip, famous car

4. House: Dreamed house, many houses, a famous house

5. Tree: Illness spreading, many health issues, spiritual healing

6. Clouds: Darkness, uncertain situation, bad fame

7. Snake: A famous woman, a diva, capricious woman

8. Coffin: Difficulty in reaching your goal, end of fame, surrendering

9. Bouquet: Beauty pageant, a star, happiness spreading around

10. Scythe: End of fame, taking action, good decision

11. Whip: Famous athlete, a conflict is peacefully managed

12. Birds: Successful interview, public speaker, peaceful discussion

13. Child: Peaceful child, gifted child, great start

14. Fox: Talented worker, job promotion, false hope

15. Bear: Great financial situation, famous job, hopeful investment

17. Stork: A sense of hope and serenity, famous woman

18. Dog: Famous friends, great friends, many friends

19. Tower: A positive perspective, high ambitions, a famous past

20. Garden: Public event, famous group, Facebook group, social media

21. Mountain: Slow progression, not letting trouble get you down

22. Crossroads: On the right path, wise decision, divinely guided

23. Mice: Small wish, stressful desire, fear of fame

24. Heart: Celebrity crush, high feeling, deep love, soulmate relationship

25. Ring: Marrying a famous person, honor, dreamed partnership

26. Book: Famous book, a famous author or teacher, a secret wish

27. Letter: News you were hoping for, a message spread out, message from above

28. Man/29. Woman: Gifted person, famous people, positive person

30. Lilies: A departed loved one, an elder is watching over you

31. Sun: Wish granted, achievement, fame and success

32. Moon: Great talents, immense creativity, good reputation

33. Key: An award, a recognition, many solutions, hope

34. Fish: Great wealth, your needs are met, prospering in every way

35. Anchor: Well-established reputation, strong hope

36. Cross: Spiritual path, Karma, feeling hopeless

17. STORK

1. Rider: News of a pregnancy, moving, a change

2. Clover: Luck, lucky change, synchronicities

3. Ship: Long travel, moving overseas, migrating

4. House: Changing residence, relocation, immigrating

5. Tree: Pregnancy, health improvement, recovery

6. Clouds: Lack of focus, uncertain change, hesitation

7. Snake: two women, a change that brings trouble, tensions

8. Coffin: A negative change, a radical transformation, going away

9. Bouquet: Positive change, surprising change, a promotion, an upgrade

10. Scythe: A change for the better, a separation, a definitive ending

11. Whip: Brutal change, conflict, a painful pregnancy

12. Birds: Speaking your truth, a positive conversation, uneasy change

13. Child: New change, a baby, starting right at the beginning

14. Fox: Career change, a job promotion, an advancement

15. Bear: Big change, new boss, raise in salary, pregnant boss

16. Stars: Positive change, good times to come

18. Dog: New friend, pregnant friend, good and caring friendship

19. Tower: An elevation, a recognition, high ambition

20. Garden: A baby shower, public event, a better group, a support group

21. Mountain: A blocked change, obstacles are anticipated

22. Crossroads: A good decision, change is needed

23. Mice: Stressful change, small change, a disappointment

24. Heart: A change in the relationship, a change of feelings

25. Ring: Moving in together, commitment, agreement

26. Book: A surprising event, unknown pregnancy, unknown relocation

27. Letter: A message about a change, pregnancy test, renting contact

28. Man: An uplifting person, an elegant person, a gentleman

29. Woman: A pregnant woman, an uplifting person, a graceful woman

30. Lilies: Long-awaited change, long-awaited pregnancy, late pregnancy

31. Sun: Successful change, a victory, a solution through change

32. Moon: Successful change, a guided decision, a pregnancy

33. Key: Significant change, completion of a project

34. Fish: Financial growth, financial upgrade

35. Anchor: Secure change, long-term change

36. Cross: Difficult change, slow progression, difficult pregnancy

18. DOG

1. Rider: News from a friend, a friendly visit

2. Clover: Lucky friendship, a friend comes to the rescue, a talisman

3. Ship: Traveling with a friend, trustworthy change, a good car

4. House: Family friend, a pet, considering a friend as family

5. Tree: Protected health, growing friendship

6. Clouds: Unfaithful friend, confused friendship, a liar

7. Snake: A manipulative friend, dangerous friendship, a betrayal

8. Coffin: A friendship ends, sick pet, sick friend

9. Bouquet: Good friends, a gift or surprise from a beloved friend

10. Scythe: End of friendship, a friend goes through an accident

11. Whip: Tension with friends, an abusive friend, a sexual friend

12. Birds: Talking with a friend, friendly conversation

13. Child: New friendship, a young and naïve friend, childhood friendship

14. Fox: False friend, working with friends

15. Bear: Strong protection, trustworthy boss, a strong friendship

16. Stars: Spirit guides and angels, famous friend

17. Stork: Trustworthy change, moving in with a friend or partner

19. Tower: A friend from the past, a lifelong friendship, highly protected

20. Garden: Group of friends, support group, a network, friendly event

21. Mountain: A blocked friendship, an enemy coming between friends

22. Crossroads: A change in the nature of your friendship

23. Mice: Stressful friendship, friend with condition

24. Heart: A lover, your best friend as your partner, loyal feeling

25. Ring: Loyal and committed, an engaged friend

26. Book: A secret friendship, unknown friend, a stranger

27. Letter: Message from a friend, friendly correspondence

28. Man: A companion, a friendly man, a protector

29. Woman: A trustworthy woman, loyal, best friend

30. Lilies: An old friend, a patient friend, loyal and trustworthy

31. Sun: A good friend, a happy friendship, protection

32. Moon: Creative and gifted friend, flirtation, romantic friendship

33. Key: Solution found by a friend, an important friendship

34. Fish: A business partner, trustworthy transaction

35. Anchor: Long-term friendship, strong friendship, strong protection

36. Cross: Friend facing difficulties, a grieving friend, a priest

19. TOWER

1. Rider: Post office, an official message

2. Clover: Luck in business ventures, a casino

3. Ship: An airport, business trip, overseas authority

4. House: A flat, real state agency, municipality, a castle

5. Tree: Hospital, a nursing center, recovery, medical school

6. Clouds: Psychological disorders, confusion from the past

7. Snake: An enemy from the past, whorehouse, exotic dancer

8. Coffin: End of isolation, undertaker

9. Bouquet: Beautiful building, a shopping mall, a florist

10. Scythe: End of isolation, demolition, end of authority

11. Whip: Prison, a gymnasium, past hurts

12. Birds: Call center, telephone company, legal discussions

13. Child: Small building, adoption agency, a nursery

14. Fox: Government worker, a red brick building, conspiracy

15. Bear: Bank, a judge, financial protection

16. Stars: Famous building, cinema industry, Hollywood

17. Stork: Adoption agency, an election, a legal change

18. Dog: Priest, minister, mayor, person under oath of allegiance

20. Garden: A hospital, a group, powerful support

21. Mountain: Problems with the authorities, imprisonment

22. Crossroads: Leaving the past behind, a legal decision

23. Mice: Stressful orders, unfavorable verdict

24. Heart: An ex-lover, a lonely heart

25. Ring: A past marriage, government agreement, a divorce

26. Book: Government secret, secret service, law school

27. Letter: Official letter, laws, contract, verdict

28. Man/29. Woman: Tall, lonely, significant person from the past

30. Lilies: A senator, a priest, a man of virtue

31. Sun: Solarium, successful procedure, happy memories

32. Moon: Psychiatric hospital, mental hospital, mental institution

33. Key: Freedom, liberation, a successful legal action

34. Fish: An aquarium, a doctor, stock exchange

35. Anchor: A lighthouse, a harbor, secure legal action

36. Cross: A church, a temple, organized religion

20. GARDEN

1. Rider: An invitation, news of a party

2. Clover: Social opportunity, happy gathering

3. Ship: A cruise, being in pleasant company during a trip

4. House: A house with garden, a cottage

5. Tree: Good health, a forest, open space, healthy group

6. Clouds: Disturbing crowd, bad weather

7. Snake: Dangerous person, troublemaker

8. Coffin: Cancelled event, a dark group, undertaker

9. Bouquet: Popularity, flower garden, opportunity to be noticed

10. Scythe: Deciding in group, staying away from social events

11. Whip: Public debate, a fighting group, the opposition

12. Birds: Public speech, concert, a choir

13. Child: Small group, innocent gathering, a birthday party

14. Fox: Teamwork, false company, suspicious event

15. Bear: Big event, strong group, a chain of restaurants

16. Stars: Social ascension, social fame, night clubbing

17. Stork: A baby shower, a house warming, uplifting conference

18. Dog: Get together, a popular friend, a festive friend

19. Tower: Public building, public organization, high standards

21. Mountain: Blocked event, cancelled event

22. Crossroads: A verdict, multiple decisions

23. Mice: Loss of popularity, public irritability, stressful event

24. Heart: Social butterfly, a passionate event, loving event

25. Ring: Wedding ceremony, public agreement

26. Book: Book signing, secret social life, secret event

27. Letter: Graduation, invitation, an announcement

28. Man/29. Woman: Popular, festive, social butterfly, important event

30. Lilies: Meditation group, a birthday, an anniversary

31. Sun: Social development, a positive group

32. Moon: Public recognition, positive reputation

33. Key: Door opening, important event, important meeting

34. Fish: Financial meeting, a trade show

35. Anchor: Secure position, a safe meeting

36. Cross: Cemetery, public burden, prayer group

21. MOUNTAIN

1. Rider: Blocked message, late visit, cancelled visit

2. Clover: Uncertain issue, bad luck, unexpected blockage

3. Ship: A cancelled trip, a tiring trip, a hard trip

4. House: Distant family, isolated house, blocked property

5. Tree: Immobilization, staying in bed

6. Clouds: Procrastination, laziness, discouragement

7. Snake: Dangerous obstacle, a challenger, a rival

8. Coffin: End of obstacles, end of difficult times

9. Bouquet: Enormous surprise, heavy gift

10. Scythe: Obstacles are sliced away, dead end

11. Whip: Big violence, big argument, hard sex

12. Birds: Big conversation, delayed conversation

13. Child: Small obstacle, lonely child, stubborn child

14. Fox: Unemployment, a blocked career

15. Bear: Big obstacle, financial blockage, stubborn boss

16. Stars: Losing faith, blocked network, Internet connection issues

17. Stork: Overcoming an obstacle, seeing the positive side of things

18. Dog: Blocked friendship, abandoned friend, an enemy

19. Tower: Loneliness, entrapment, isolation, imprisonment

20. Garden: Delayed meeting, a "persona non grata"

22. Crossroads: Difficult decision, procrastinating, stubborn decision

23. Mice: Removal of obstacle, losing faith, a hill

24. Heart: Feeling of loneliness, feeling abandoned, a depression

25. Ring: An obligation, strong marriage, stalemated relationship

26. Book: A big secret, a big book, a hard apprenticeship

27. Letter: Difficult news, long-awaited information

28. Man: A lonely man, a stubborn person, an enemy

29. Woman: A lonely woman, a stubborn person, an enemy

30. Lilies: A major setback, a long delay, being patient

31. Sun: Delays are over, a positive outcome

32. Moon: Big emotion, psychic blocks, feeling lost

33. Key: Solutions are found, successfully overcoming an obstacle

34. Fish: Financial blocks, overspending

35. Anchor: Long-term blockage, a resistant enemy

36. Cross: Burdens, hardship, trouble, worries

22. CROSSROADS

1. Rider: A visitor coming forward, news on the road

2. Clover: Lucky decision, finding a way, a positive issue

3. Ship: Deciding where to travel, road itinerary, multiple trips

4. House: Two houses, decision about a house, family decision

5. Tree: Health decision, deciding for your well-being

6. Clouds: Uncertain decision, multiple decisions, hesitation

7. Snake: Dangerous woman, troublesome path, enemy at the corner

8. Coffin: A negative decision, a dark decision, a negative turn

9. Bouquet: Multiple gifts, surprising decision, beautiful path

10. Scythe: A final decision, road accident, a decisive turn

11. Whip: Multiple sex partners, painful path, painful decision

12. Birds: Conversation that leads to a decision, many voices

13. Child: Small decision, deciding to start things fresh

14. Fox: Work decision, multiple jobs, cunning decision

15. Bear: Big decision, multiple sources of income

16. Stars: Many decisions, guided decision, positive decision

17. Stork: Good direction, things get better

18. Dog: A separation, going away, a friend takes distance

19. Tower: Legal decision, choose only one

20. Garden: Multiple groups, rural setting, two events

21. Mountain: A blocked path, meeting many obstacles on the way

23. Mice: Stressful decision, poor decision, small decision

24. Heart: Heartfelt decision, listen to your heart, conflicting emotion

25. Ring: Going round in circles, marriage or relationship ends

26. Book: Secret decision, a discovery, two lessons

27. Letter: A correspondence is on its way, multiple documents

28. Man/29. Woman: Indecisive, independent, decision maker

30. Lilies: Wise choice, peaceful decision, two elderly people

31. Sun: Positive choice, best action, successful turn

32. Moon: Creative choice, emotional decision, difficult choice

33. Key: Important decision, successful turn, new opening

34. Fish: Financial decision, action plan, money coming

35. Anchor: Stable and secure choice, a long-term decision

36. Cross: Many burdens, troublesome path, a difficult choice

23. MICE

1. Rider: Stressful visit, stressful news, news of a loss	
2. Clover: Bad luck, misfortune, missing an opportunity	
3. Ship: Broken car, stressful trip, small journey	
4. House: House reparation, stressful family situation	
5. Tree: Cancer, any disease that eats away, loss of good health	
6. Clouds: Confusion, stressful situation, nothing seems to work	
7. Snake: Big trouble, danger, a petite woman, envious person	
8. Coffin: End of worries, end of the dark tunnel, finding a way out	
9. Bouquet: Lost gift, unpleasant surprise, a robbery	
10. Scythe: End of stress, a radical decision	
11. Whip: A painful loss, moral harassment, small argument	
12. Birds: Stressful conversation, stressful couple	
13. Child: Stressed and anxious child, small loss	
14. Fox: Parasite, taking everything you have, losing your job	
15. Bear: Big stress, financial loss, weight loss, a fraudulent boss	
16. Stars: Finding a missing item, the robbery expands	
17. Stork: Small progress, stressful move, stressful pregnancy	
18. Dog: Anxious friend, a thief, losing a friend, sick dog	
19. Tower: Trouble with the authorities, accused of fraud	
20. Garden: Stressful event, a draining group, pickpocketing	
21. Mountain: Stressful blockage, frustration, feeling trapped	
22. Crossroads: Stressful decision, frustrating choice	
24. Heart: Feeling lost, anxious heart, losing someone you love	
25. Ring: Missing jewelry, a separation, a breakup	
26. Book: A secret is slowly discovered, unknown worries	
27. Letter: Missing document, stressful message, a bill	
28. Man/29. Woman: Missing person, stressed, worried, frightened, illness	
30. Lilies: Losing your peace, age-related health issues	
31. Sun: Recovering a lost object, burnout, trying too hard	
32. Moon: Anxiety, stress, depression	
33. Key: A breakthrough, a solution, finding answers	
34. Fish: Money loss, stressful financial situation, a financial fraud	
35. Anchor: Long-term stress, unemployment, hitting rock bottom	
36. Cross: Grief, loss, a hard situation	

24. HEART

1. Rider: A lovely visit, romantic news, a lover

2. Clover: Love at first sight, the heart chakra

3. Ship: Romantic trip, a honeymoon, long-distance relationship

4. House: Lovely home, love from the family

5. Tree: Heart disease, a growing love

6. Clouds: A confused heart, uncertain love

7. Snake: An affair, the mistress, the other woman, a rival

8. Coffin: A relationship ends, hating or disliking someone

9. Bouquet: Beautiful relationship, surprising feeling

10. Scythe: Heart surgery, end of a relationship, heartbreak

11. Whip: Passion and sex, violent emotion, argument

12. Birds: A married couple, romantic conversation

13. Child: New love, young lover, a teenage crush

14. Fox: A liar, dishonest person, a passionate job

15. Bear: Overbearing partner, wealthy partner, loving boss

16. Stars: Dreamed partner, soulmate, Mr./Mrs. Right

17. Stork: Love that gives you wings, positive relationship

18. Dog: Loving friend, best friends can become lovers, soulmates

19. Tower: A lonely heart, fortress around your heart

20. Garden: Multiple partners, flirtation, public romantic declaration

21. Mountain: A heart to conquer, a blocked heart, a lonely heart

22. Crossroads: Love related choice, heartfelt decision, two lovers

23. Mice: A grieving heart, anxiety and stress, feeling lost, ex-lover

25. Ring: A partnership, marriage of love, heart-shaped ring

26. Book: Secret feeling, hidden affair, secret crush

27. Letter: Love letter, a written declaration, a Valentine card

28. Man/29. Woman: Loving, passionate, true feeling, totally in love

30. Lilies: Patient heart, an old love, can represent your first love

31. Sun: True feelings, warm feeling of love, successful relationship

32. Moon: Romance, a deep love, romantic evening

33. Key: A significant lover, true emotion, true love

34. Fish: Lots of emotion, love of money, deep love

35. Anchor: Deep love, long-term relationship, togetherness

36. Cross: A heavy heart, painful feelings, past life lover

25. RING

1. Rider: News about a partnership, wedding announcement

2. Clover: Lucky partnership, a positive marriage

3. Ship: Honeymoon, traveling to attend a marriage

4. House: The town hall, real estate contract

5. Tree: Healthy marriage, growing relationship

6. Clouds: Uncertain partnership, the marriage goes through a storm

7. Snake: Troubled partnership, a jealous and abusive partner

8. Coffin: Ending a partnership, troubled relationship

9. Bouquet: A wedding proposal, beautiful wedding

10. Scythe: A divorce, a breakup, a definite separation

11. Whip: Domestic argument, rocky relationship, abusive partner

12. Birds: The couple, marital conversation, talking about a contract

13. Child: New partner, marrying someone with children, adoption

14. Fox: Cunning partnership, job commitment, suspicious agreement

15. Bear: Big wealthy marriage, getting married for financial reasons

16. Stars: Promising marriage, famous wedding

17. Stork: Modifying a contract, unsure commitment

18. Dog: A partner, business associates, a trustworthy person

19. Tower: Court, legal agreement, bridal store, a jeweler

20. Garden: Public agreement, outdoor wedding ceremony, the guests

21. Mountain: Trouble with a contract, a difficult partnership, an enemy

22. Crossroads: Turning in circles, a separation, a split, double life

23. Mice: End of a relationship or a partnership, a stolen ring

24. Heart: Loving partnership, united loving couple

26. Book: Secret partnership, secret marriage, deal kept secret

27. Letter: Wedding invitation, wedding certificate, contract

28. Man: A married, committed man, a husband, a fiancé

29. Woman: A married, committed woman, a wife, a fiancée

30. Lilies: Old partnership, marrying a virgin, trustworthy relationship

31. Sun: Successful partnership, bright future, successful deal

32. Moon: A pattern, a cycle, strong attraction, romance

33. Key: Significant partnership, important contract, a big "yes"

34. Fish: Business agreement, financial commitment

35. Anchor: Commitment, secure partnership, lifelong marriage

36. Cross: Painful relationship, difficult contract, painful commitment

26. BOOK

1. Rider: Unknown visitor, news about a secret

2. Clover: Unexpected discovery, lucky information, a green book

3. Ship: Passport, secret travel, unknown destination

4. House: Family secret, discreet family, unknown property

5. Tree: Health education, research on the family tree

6. Clouds: Confusing secret, a veil of mystery, a confusing book

7. Snake: A lie, a secret woman, a dangerous secret

8. Coffin: Unknown danger, a secret is known, end of study

9. Bouquet: Doubly nice surprise, secret gift, beautiful book

10. Scythe: A secret revealed that leads to action, end of schooling

11. Whip: A bothersome secret, sex book, sex education

12. Birds: A conference, an educational speech, arguments

13. Child: A studious child, small secret, new information, new study

14. Fox: Detective, an officer, an executive, secret agent, bookkeeper

15. Bear: Big secret, checkbook, cookbook, secret investment

16. Stars: Astronomy, esoteric study, astrology, a secret spreads out

17. Stork: Midwife, change in study, secret move, secret pregnancy

18. Dog: Obstetrician, study mate, smart friend, educated person

19. Tower: University, law school, a prestigious establishment

20. Garden: Social studies, workshop, group study, botanical study

21. Mountain: A pause in your schedule, a sabbatical year, a blockage

22. Crossroads: Deciding on your academic path, multiple lessons

23. Mice: A known secret, secret from the past, stressful studies

24. Heart: Secret admirer, a secret relationship, a crush

25. Ring: Secret relationship, secret alliance, hidden jewelry

27. Letter: Secret information, a license, a diploma, secret letter

28. Man: Secret man, educated man, intelligent man

29. Woman: Secret woman, educated woman, intelligent woman

30. Lilies: Long studies, old secret, an expert, in some cases a lawyer

31. Sun: Successful apprenticeship, a graduation, a secret is revealed

32. Moon: Art studies, PhD, psychology, therapy, poetry

33. Key: Important secret, important studies, a secret is unlocked

34. Fish: Financial secret, commercial school, marketing studies

35. Anchor: A sealed secret, long-term apprenticeship, working hard

36. Cross: Spiritual studies, overwhelming studies, hard course

27. LETTER

1. Rider: The postman, messages, someone coming with an invitation

2. Clover: Lottery ticket, St. Patrick card, tombola ticket

3. Ship: Flight ticket, visa, overseas correspondence, driver's license

4. House: Real estate contract, news from a relative, correspondence

5. Tree: A diagnosis, blood analysis results, X-ray results

6. Clouds: Bad news, confusing news, a blocked (momentarily unavailable) letter

7. Snake: Letter from a woman, negative information

8. Coffin: A final notice, a separation letter, a closure

9. Bouquet: Beautiful letter, surprising news, positive news

10. Scythe: Decisive information, end of communication

11. Whip: A complaint, sexual messages, dirty messages

12. Birds: Pouring your heart in a letter, reading aloud a letter

13. Child: New letter, a memo, birth announcement, SMS

14. Fox: A treat, blackmail, a disclosure, a writer

15. Bear: Credit card, thick letter, invoice, bank statement

16. Stars: SMS, MMS, email, virtual messages, many messages

17. Stork: Birth announcement, news in the air, notice of departure

18. Dog: Loyalty card, friendly letter, news about a friend

19. Tower: Post office, long letter, legal document

20. Garden: Party invitation, concert ticket, public messages

21. Mountain: Belated correspondence, a block document

22. Crossroads: News on its way, two letters, a reminder

23. Mice: A lost letter, a small note, a negative letter, a bill

24. Heart: Love letter, a message for a date, a declaration of love

25. Ring: A wedding invitation, letter from an associate

26. Book: Folders, book, secret document, hidden document

28. Man: Writer, blogger, receptive, message from a man

29. Woman: Writer, blogger, receptive, message from a woman

30. Lilies: Christmas card, message from an elder, old document

31. Sun: Fantastic news, positive information, a bright letter

32. Moon: A poem, romantic message, creative writing

33. Key: Important document, significant piece of information

34. Fish: Business news, business document, business correspondence

35. Anchor: A letter for sure, a document of confirmation

36. Cross: Messages from above, bad news, hard news

28. MAN AND 29. WOMAN

1. Rider: Another man, a visit, someone just passing

2. Clover: A time of luck and opportunity for the querent

3. Ship: A change coming along, the querent may be a foreigner

4. House: The querent's property, belonging and family

5. Tree: The querent may have some health issues

6. Clouds: The querent is going through a time of confusion

7. Snake: Another woman, the querent may be afflicted by jealousy

8. Coffin: The querent is going through a phase of transformation

9. Bouquet: Charming, attractive person, the querent can expect a gift

10. Scythe: The querent is going through a time of decision-making

11. Whip: The querent is experiencing a time of argument and violence

12. Birds: The querent is someone that communicates easily

13. Child: The querent is going through a time of new beginnings

14. Fox: Cunning, the querent's question involves work and career

15. Bear: The querent enjoys a good position, he is respected

16. Stars: Well-known people, inspiring and bright personality

17. Stork: Graceful and uplifting personality, a positive change

18. Dog: Loyal and faithful, friendship is important to the querent

19. Tower: Ambitious, the querent is fortifying walls around him/herself

20. Garden: Festive and social, the querent is single

21. Mountain: Stubborn and lonely, the querent should keep his distance

22. Crossroads: The querent is going through a time of indecision

23. Mice: Stressed and anxious, the querent is going through a loss

24. Heart: Passionate and charming, the querent is in love

25. Ring: Committed, the querent is already involved in a relationship

26. Book: Secretive and smart, the querent is involved in a secret

27. Letter: Eloquent, the querent will receive a piece of information

30. Lilies: Wise and mature the querent is a spiritual person

31. Sun: Happy and optimistic, the querent is successful in everything

32. Moon: The querent will be recognized for who she/he is

33. Key: Successful person, experiencing a lot of breakthroughs

34. Fish: The querent is wealthy and involved in business transactions

35. Anchor: Stable and focused, the querent is reliable

36. Cross: Drained and tired, the querent is going through difficulties

30. LILIES

1. Rider: Old message, visit from an elder, peaceful visitor

2. Clover: Lucky elderly man, elder with green eyes

3. Ship: An old car, a peaceful journey, a winter trip, a green car

4. House: Old house, the elders, peaceful home

5. Tree: Long recovery, age-related health issues

6. Clouds: Confused mind, brothers, two men, uncertain man

7. Snake: Negative elder woman, manipulative woman

8. Coffin: A widower, peaceful ending, a retirement

9. Bouquet: A couple, flirtation, attraction, seduction

10. Scythe: Retirement, a stressful situation, old wounds

11. Whip: Very slow action, old argument, old conflict

12. Birds: Old couple, old conversation, long conversation

13. Child: Grandfather, elder child, innocent person, a patriarch

14. Fox: Untrustworthy, old career, cunning old person, an old timer

15. Bear: Retirement fund, a pension, a matriarch

16. Stars: Famous elderly man, peaceful night, ancestors

17. Stork: Positive change, slow change, positive move

18. Dog: A priest, lifelong friendship, trusted friend, old pet

19. Tower: High authority, a trusted authority figure

20. Garden: Retirement party, late gathering, a get-together

21. Mountain: Non activity, everything is slowed down and blocked

22. Crossroads: Long-time decision, wise choice, two elders

23. Mice: Sclerosis, cancer, disease that eats away

24. Heart: Mature love, an old romance, a loving elder, trusted heart

25. Ring: Old or late marriage, an old association, old contract

26. Book: Great wisdom, old secret, vintage book

27. Letter: Vintage document, old news, peaceful news

28. Man: Spiritual, trustworthy, patient, old

29. Woman: Spiritual, trustworthy, patient, old

31. Sun: Success at last, happy ending, a positive outcome

32. Moon: A creative man, an artist, a recognized figure

33. Key: A solution is found, patience is key, a long-term solution

34. Fish: Old business venture, a lifelong source of income

35. Anchor: Stable and long-term situation

36. Cross: Old burden, the wait is hard, impatience

31. SUN

1. Rider: Good news, a wonderful visit, fast movement

2. Clover: Big luck, jackpot, synchronicity

3. Ship: Successful trip, a positive change, a bright journey

4. House: A happy family, the perfect house, luminous home

5. Tree: Good health, improvement, healing, a recovery

6. Clouds: Trouble success, an unexpected situation

7. Snake: Successful woman, dangerous success, envious woman

8. Coffin: Positive ending, a metamorphosis, a positive change

9. Bouquet: A shiny gift, a positive combo, happiness and joy

10. Scythe: A positive decision, positive ending

11. Whip: Competition, pleasant sex, burnout

12. Birds: Positive conversation, uplifting speech

13. Child: New beginnings, bright start, hyperactive child

14. Fox: Successful job, succeeding using unconventional way

15. Bear: Strong conviction, fortunate situation, good investment

16. Stars: An award, a recognition, an acknowledgment, a reward

17. Stork: Positive change, going to a warm place, positive move

18. Dog: Trusted friend, a radiant friend, best friend

19. Tower: A safe place, electric company, protection

20. Garden: Successful event, positive environment, bright group

21. Mountain: A positive breakthrough, overcoming a difficult time

22. Crossroads: Good decision, divinely guided, positive direction

23. Mice: Burnout, loss of energy and vitality, extreme stress

24. Heart: Good feelings, successful love life, passion

25. Ring: Positive relationship, great deal, wonderful union

26. Book: A secret is revealed, successful scholarship

27. Letter: Great news, right document, right information

28. Man: Brilliant, optimistic, successful, positive

29. Woman: Brilliant, optimistic, successful, positive

30. Lilies: An awaited success, positive old person, a good man

32. Moon: Harmony, an attraction, mood, creative ideas

33. Key: Great success, doorway to prosperity, brilliant solution

34. Fish: Midas touch, lucky hit, great transaction, abundance

35. Anchor: Hitting the mark, reaching a milestone, a realization

36. Cross: God, a miracle, a blessing in disguise

32. MOON

1. Rider: Emotive visit, emotive news

2. Clover: Good fortune, lucky charm

3. Ship: Romantic trip, a creative journey, traveling by night

4. House: Creative home, creative studio, workshop

5. Tree: Hormones, mental health, your mood, your thoughts

6. Clouds: Confusing emotion, stubborn, afraid to decide

7. Snake: Known as being manipulative and envious

8. Coffin: Lack of creativity, lack of emotion, not romantic at all

9. Bouquet: Beautiful artwork, masterpiece, a romance

10. Scythe: Emotional breakup, an emotional ending

11. Whip: Sexual fantasy, argument that leads to hate

12. Birds: Romantic couple, deep communication

13. Child: A creative child, a pregnancy

14. Fox: Creative work, a psychic, a medium

15. Bear: Mother, acknowledgment by your boss, full moon

16. Stars: Fame and recognition, a dream come true

17. Stork: A pregnancy, creative new change

18. Dog: Well-known friend, creative partner, romantic companion

19. Tower: Self-sabotage, delusion, entrapment

20. Garden: Public recognition, creative group, a workshop

21. Mountain: Lack of creativity, a blockage, a standstill

22. Crossroads: Creative choice, intuitive decision

23. Mice: Lost of recognition, insecurity, anxiety

24. Heart: Highly sensitive, a romance

25. Ring: Creative partnership, a true engagement, a proposal

26. Book: Secret romance, creative study

27. Letter: Romantic letter, creative letter, romantic messages

28. Man: Romantic, creative, recognized, artistic

29. Woman: Romantic, creative, recognized, artistic

30. Lilies: Relationship with an older person, powerful connection

31. Sun: Fame, successful recognition, bright artwork

33. Key: Significant creation, successful recognition

34. Fish: Financial growth, creative business

35. Anchor: Longlasting romance, emotional stability

36. Cross: Religious art, creative burden, anxiety

33. KEY

1. Rider: Important message, an important visitor

2. Clover: Lucky event, handy solution, perfect timing

3. Ship: Important trip, a successful journey, car keys

4. House: House keys, important family, significant house

5. Tree: Key to healing, recovery, therapy

6. Clouds: Uncertain success, confused outcome

7. Snake: Danger, jealousy toward your success, a successful woman

8. Coffin: Significant ending, a door closes and another one opens

9. Bouquet: Key to joy and happiness, a successful woman

10. Scythe: Important decision, doing the right thing

11. Whip: Best sex, important conflict, argument

12. Birds: Best conversation, successful discussion

13. Child: Promising beginning, important child

14. Fox: Significant job, success through manipulation

15. Bear: Good boss, financial success, door to prosperity

16. Stars: Great success, powerful guidance, important dream

17. Stork: Positive change, successful move

18. Dog: Successful friendship, significant friend

19. Tower: Successful legal procedures, organization is key

20. Garden: Important meeting, significant event, important group

21. Mountain: Major block, important delays, be patient here

22. Crossroads: On the right path, best options, important choice

23. Mice: Distraction, not able to focus, worries, stressful situation

24. Heart: Soulmate relations, key to your heart, significant feeling

25. Ring: Successful alliance, important contact, an agreement

26. Book: Successful studies, focus on theory, a secret is revealed

27. Letter: Important mail, important document, news of a success

28. Man: Important, successful, handy

29. Woman: Important, successful, handy

30. Lilies: Wisdom is key, patience is key, virtue is key

31. Sun: Big success, key to success, a victory, good over evil

32. Moon: Masterpiece, intuition is key

34. Fish: Important investment, significant transaction

35. Anchor: Definite success, significant milestone

36. Cross: A sacrifice, spiritual connection

34. FISH

1. Rider: Financial news, a salesman, new transaction

2. Clover: Good business, lucky transaction, financial luck

3. Ship: Overseas transaction, traveling for business, swift trip

4. House: Home-based business, family business, real estate business

5. Tree: Financial growth, health business, dehydration

6. Clouds: Confused business, trouble transaction, uncertain business

7. Snake: An enemy in the business, dangerous transaction

8. Coffin: Bankruptcy, closing a business, dead transaction

9. Bouquet: Beauty sales representative, good transaction

10. Scythe: End of transaction, business decision, a cut in finance

11. Whip: Money argument, repetitive sales or client

12. Birds: Consulting business, wealthy couple, business discussion

13. Child: New transaction, small sales, small purchase

14. Fox: Entrepreneur, a fraud, a well-paid job

15. Bear: Big investment, a large purchase, wealthy boss

16. Stars: Many transactions, multiple businesses, dreamed transaction

17. Stork: Financial change, business relocation, positive transaction

18. Dog: Trustworthy transaction, wealthy friend, pet business

19. Tower: Financial institution, store, a mall, water company

20. Garden: Customers, grouped sales, product presentation

21. Mountain: Blocked transaction, financial blockage

22. Crossroads: Business decision, two sales or purchases

23. Mice: Small business, financial loss, stressful business

24. Heart: Donation, charity, love of money

25. Ring: Wealthy marriage, business agreement, purchasing a ring

26. Book: Secret transaction, unknown business, business studies

27. Letter: Business exchange, business correspondence, tax, invoice

28. Man: Businessman, wealthy man, entrepreneur, independent

29. Woman: Businesswoman, wealthy woman, entrepreneur, independent

30. Lilies: Retirement, slow transaction, establishing a business

31. Sun: Successful business, positive transaction

32. Moon: Art industry, creative transaction, positive business

33. Key: Successful sales, important transaction

35. Anchor: Long-term wealth, secure transaction

36. Cross: Financial burden, negative transaction

35. ANCHOR

1. Rider: Safe visit, new goals

2. Clover: Long-term fortune, good fortune

3. Ship: Reaching an important milestone, an achievement

4. House: Stable family, secure family, security

5. Tree: Strong health, stable health, recovery

6. Clouds: Uncertain foundation, shaky foundation, confusing goals

7. Snake: Trouble, not secure, dangerous goal

8. Coffin: End of security, a danger, lack of support

9. Bouquet: Long-term happiness, positive situation

10. Scythe: Sudden change, end of stability

11. Whip: Long-lasting conflict, an addiction, a settle pattern

12. Birds: Safe conversation, lengthy discussion, lifelong couple

13. Child: New goal, safe child, small goal

14. Fox: Long-term job, job with objectives, secure position

15. Bear: Powerful, big goal, strong determination

16. Stars: Achieving your goals, working on your dreams

17. Stork: Steady change, settling elsewhere, a positive change

18. Dog: Safe friend, strong friendship, lifelong friendship

19. Tower: Long life, high goal, high perspective

20. Garden: Safe group, working with the public

21. Mountain: Going nowhere, being stuck, huge obstacle

22. Crossroads: Choosing security, a permanent decision

23. Mice: Stressful situation, your foundations are slowly falling apart

24. Heart: Strong feeling, faithfulness, a profound love

25. Ring: Solid marriage, a solid commitment, long-term relationship

26. Book: Research, looking deeper, investigating, hard study

27. Letter: Work document, an SOS, a paperweight

28. Man: Secure, stable, strong, determined, hard worker

29. Woman: Secure, stable, strong, determined, hard worker

30. Lilies: Retirement, loyal, someone you can trust

31. Sun: Successful job, attaining your goals, protection

32. Moon: Strong insight, a hard worker, established reputation

33. Key: Successful achievement, significant goal

34. Fish: Financial security, secure transaction

36. Cross: Long-term worry, deep pain, anchored burden

36. CROSS

1. Rider: Difficult news, painful visit

2. Clover: Bad luck, misfortune

3. Ship: A sad journey, retreat, a troubled trip

4. House: A church, burden at home, conflicted house

5. Tree: Troubled health, pain, incurable disease

6. Clouds: Spiritual conflict, heavy confusion

7. Snake: A big danger, things getting worse

8. Coffin: End of worry, a transformation

9. Bouquet: Spiritual gift, an offering of flowers

10. Scythe: Accident, severe injury, sudden pain

11. Whip: Physical abuse, sexual abuse, hard times

12. Birds: Heavy conversation, argument, unhappy couple

13. Child: A baptism, a bullied child, a troubled child

14. Fox: Burden at work, abusive person

15. Bear: An abusive boss, financial downfall

16. Stars: Prayer, keeping the faith, asking for help

17. Stork: Worrying about change, an amelioration

18. Dog: A priest, a counselor, a difficult friendship

19. Tower: Organized religion, spiritual center

20. Garden: Public sorrow, prayer group, counseling group

21. Mountain: Enormous obstacle, overburdened, no way out

22. Crossroads: Difficult decision, painful choice

23. Mice: Heavy debt, financial problems, stressful situation

24. Heart: Heartache, a twin flame, destined love

25. Ring: Unhappy marriage, a difficult contract, painful agreement

26. Book: Religious study, religious secrets, sacred books

27. Letter: Painful messages, difficult information

28. Man: Religious, unhappy, drained, burdened

29. Woman: Religious, unhappy, drained, burdened

30. Lilies: Burden and pain associated with old age

31. Sun: A relief, help will come, a recovery

32. Moon: Self-sacrifice, depression, a hard time

33. Key: Destiny, an important lesson, success at last

34. Fish: Deep pain, difficult transaction, hard business

35. Anchor: Long-term suffering, hard work, spiritual work

SPIRITUAL READING WITH LENORMAND

"DISCIPLINE ENABLED THE ANGELS
TO BE IMMACULATE AND HOLY."
—RUMI

Many do not realize that the Lenormand cards can also be used in spiritual consultations. I have noticed that readers from Brazil and Mexico use them in their practices and readings this way. I have been reading the spiritual nuances in Lenormand cards for a very long time, and as you saw in previous chapters, for individual card meanings, I provide both card messages (advice) and the Archangel for each card to help you in your spiritual readings.

I've been working with the Angelic realm for a long time as well. Like many people, I once believed that angels were myth, and if they existed they would belong to an organized religion. Little did I know that I would encounter one in my life, in one of my most surprising yet life-threatening moments. Here is my story with the angels.

In my thirties, my private practice was growing bigger, and readings took a lot of my time; I quit my job as an assistant manager so that I could focus only on my spiritual work. During this period, there were intense family issues in my life, which seriously disturbed my contentment and peacefulness. I was at the edge of depression and was unable to sleep. I felt miserable and called for God's help, begging him for a miracle. I hoped that this state I was in was not a handicap in my performing readings for others; providing readings was actually the only thing that gave me peace. One day, on my way to give a group reading, I fell asleep at the wheel. My car slid off the road and descended down a 98 ½-foot (thirty meter) cliff. During the free fall, an opalescent, luminous green emerald light being was suddenly sitting next to me in the passenger seat. I felt warm, peaceful, joyful, a state I had never experienced before. I said to the being: "Who are you?" The reply was a reassuring echoed voice in my head: "I am Archangel Raphael. Everything is fine. You are safe." Miraculously, I was! The car hit bottom, and I was able to get myself free and leave the accident with only minor scrapes and bruises.

I knew what had just happened was extraordinary, and I had to understand it better, to investigate. A week after the accident, I noticed that during my sessions, my gifts were amplified; I began seeing orbs of light around people. I discovered that these spheres were actually angels who were assisting and helping those people. At first I marveled at this, and then I was scared that the accident had caused a trauma that resulted in hallucinations. So I called my doctor right away and was checked by a specialist.

I underwent a brain scan, and the examination revealed that everything was perfectly normal. I decided to explore the changes, and discovered that I could communicate directly with the angels and receive guidance on how to create a happy and successful life; I started with myself. I immediately incorporated the angel's advice in my Lenormand readings and received immense guidance both for myself and my clients. It all served to take my readings up a notch, literally.

Today, I've assigned an Archangel to each Lenormand card based on the Archangels' shared expertise. The Archangels are powerful divine beings that can be at different places and with different people simultaneously. They are here to help you with any area of your life and provide you with powerful guidance to help you live a peaceful and meaningful life. Know this.

The ten archangels I worked closely with are **Azrael, Chamuel, Gabriel, Jophiel, Haniel, Metatron, Michael, Raguel, Raphael, and Uriel.** You will notice that some of the cards are aligned to a guardian angel instead of an archangel. The Archangels and Guardian Angels are trustworthy, and it is safe for you to call upon and work with them. Here is an introduction to each one.

AZRAEL

Azrael is one of the most beautiful angels and the most misunderstood. He is known as "Angel of Grief," or "Angel of Death." He is the angel that guides souls to heaven after their crossing. He then consoles the survivors and helps them heal from grief.

WHEN TO CALL ON ARCHANGEL AZRAEL

Call upon Azrael when you are facing loss, death, and transition. He will help you overcome any hard situation and the drama that goes with it.

CHAMUEL

Chamuel's name means "The Eyes of God"; he has the ability to see everything and can help you recover anything you have lost. Another mission of Chamuel is the manifestation of universal Peace; he brings peacefulness to any situation you are dealing with.

WHEN TO CALL ON ARCHANGEL CHAMUEL

Call upon Chamuel to help you find whatever you are seeking in your life: from a soulmate relationship, to a new job, to a new home.

GABRIEL

Gabriel is the famous angel of annunciation; he is the trusted messenger of God. He is the only angel that uses verbal communication. Gabriel is the one that helps in matters of child conception, pregnancy, and adoption. He is also the angel to writers.

WHEN TO CALL ON ARCHANGEL GABRIEL

Call upon Gabriel in all areas of child-rearing. For work matters, he can open doors of opportunity for you and help you on your career path.

HANIEL

Haniel's name means "Grace/Joy of God," and she is the archangel aligned to the moon and its magic. In ancient Babylon, she was one of the archangels who guided the priest-astronomers with their work in astrology, astronomy, divination, and spiritual healing. In my personal experience, Haniel had been for me the angel of intuition; when I called upon her during a reading, I would find myself in a highthen intuitive state.

WHEN TO CALL ON ARCHANGEL HANIEL

Call upon Haniel whenever you need guidance; like the moon brightly shining in the dark night, Haniel will surround you with her magical lunar energy putting you in a state of great psychic awareness. She can also help you get out or arase a cyclic pattern.

JOPHIEL

Jophiel is known as the "Angel of Beauty." Even though the angels do not have physical form or genders and their energy tends to be both masculine and feminine, Jophiel has a distinctive feminine energy.

WHEN TO CALL ON ARCHANGEL JOPHIEL

Call upon Jophiel to help you see things in a detached perspective. She can help you uplift your thoughts, reduce clutter, and balance your space.

METATRON

Archangel Metatron is one of the archangels believed to have lived a human life before ascending to the archangel domain as a reward for a pious and exemplary life. He is the scribe of God and stands very close to him. He is an expert in sacred geometry and a teacher of esoteric knowledge. He is also the angel of the indigo children.

WHEN TO CALL ON ARCHANGEL METATRON

Call upon Metatron to clear and balance your chakras. He can also help you if your life mission involves healing and helping sensitive children.

MICHAEL

Archangel Michael is a sainted archangel and one of the most popular. Michael's name means "Who is like God." He is known to be a warrior, fighting for justice and balance.

WHEN TO CALL ON ARCHANGEL MICHAEL

Call upon Michael whenever you feel you need extra protection. He makes sure that your house, belongings, loved ones, and you are safe and protected. He knows about everyone life's mission, and he can help you find yours as well.

RAGUEL

Archangel Raguel is the angel who harmonizes relationships and who brings wonderful new people into your life. His name means "Friend of God."

WHEN TO CALL ON ARCHANGEL RAGUEL

You can ask Raguel for help and guidance with any relationship, and he will bring peace to the situation quickly.

RAPHAEL

Archangel Raphael is another sainted archangel; his name means "God Heals." I see him as the divine doctor who can lead you to both physical and emotional healing. He is the one who knows about our soulmate and how to connect with them.

WHEN TO CALL ON ARCHANGEL RAPHAEL

Call upon Raphael when you need healing for yourself or a loved one; he will instantly fly and surround you with his healing green emerald light. Traveling is the perfect time to call upon him for a smooth trip, as he is the patron saint of travelers.

URIEL

Archangel Uriel is the "of Enlightenment" who illuminates our mind with information, ideas, epiphanies, and insights.

WHEN TO CALL ON ARCHANGEL URIEL

Call upon Uriel when you are attending a test or examination; he will help you focus and drive away the anxiety and stress. I like to call upon Uriel each time I am starting a new project.

GUARDIAN ANGELS

We all have guardian angels with us at all times, no matter what religion or background we come from. Guardian angels are divine messengers that are here to assist us in everything that we do, from paying a bill, to finding lost keys, to meeting your soulmate. Any time you need help with something, call on your guardian angel and she/he will fly to your rescue.

WHEN TO CALL ON YOUR GUARDIAN ANGEL

Guardian angels can help with everything. There is no mission too small or too big for them; they are available to us 24/7. You must do only this: acknowledge and give them permission to help you, as they cannot violate the law of free will.

PHYSICAL ATTRIBUTES WITH LENORMAND

"APPEAR AS YOU ARE, BE AS YOU APPEAR."
—RUMI

Lenormand can be used in describing people based on physical appearance. In psychic readings, the number one question is usually love-related, and the question I often hear is "What does my soulmate look like?"

Lenormand can reply to this question with amazing accuracy. It can help you recognize a particular person who may be directly influencing your reading or question. Oftentimes in the scenario of life, there are multiple actors; some will play a major role and influence you in positive as well as in negative ways, while others will play a minor role.

When pulling cards to describe someone's appearance, focus on the descriptive side of the cards, not the general meaning or the combination of the cards. For instance, the Fox 14 will describe someone with red hair, rather than a cunning person. Another one, the Bear 15 will describe someone hairy with extra weight, rather than cash flow or investment.

I want to share a personal story with you about a reading I did for a client named Adeline. She is a divorced mum of a seven-year-old boy. It had been four years since her divorce and she felt ready to date. Her question was, "Will I meet someone?" I cast The Grand Tableau for her, and it was obvious that she would find love but, before finding Mr. Right, she would be dating two other guys. Then she asked, "How will I know, who's who?" and I told her that I would describe them one by one so that she would easily know. I usually pull three cards to describe someone's physical attributes, so we started with contender number one.

She pulled:
Ship 3, Rider 1, Tower 19
I said: "He is someone with tanned skin (Ship), possibly a foreigner (Rider), fit, slender, tall, with flat chest (Tower)."

For contender number two, she pulled:
Bear 15, Garden 20, Birds 12
The cards show that he is someone with extra weight, hairy (Bear), but quite attractive, well-groomed (Garden), with small eyes (Bird).

For Mr. Right, we got:

Tree 5, Fox 14, Clover 2

It was clear that Mr. Right had green eyes (confirmed here by both Tree and Clover), red hair (Fox), with an elegant walking style (Fox). I also got the feeling that Mr. Right would have some Irish background.

Adeline recorded the reading with her phone, and she promised to let me know how accurate things were as they unfolded. Two weeks later, I received a text message from Adeline:

Contender one is here. As you've said, he is a foreigner; he is from Morocco, fit, slender, with nice, tan skin.

I smiled as I read the message.

Three month later, I received another message, and this time with a picture that clearly validated the reading. The guy really looked bear-like, a bit on the hairy side, but nicely dressed. You could see that he had good taste, and his eyes were piercing, just like those of the Birds card.

Six months later I received a call from Adeline requesting a reading session; on the day of her reading, Adeline came accompanied. She introduced me to the man who came with her: "Alexandre, here is Kevin a.k.a. Mr. Right, and Kevin, here's the man who had predicted your arrival." It was a funny moment; Kevin was Irish, green eyes, red hair, and at the time of this writing, Kevin had proposed to Adeline. She said "Yes," another thing Lenormand predicted—but this is another story.

I must point out that the reading didn't sabotage the relationship; Adeline gave each one their chance, but she reported that they were not compatible. I think that knowing in advance about an event helps you live it fully. Nothing is written in stone, I believe that the destiny of our lives is written in pencil, and we have the eraser to change and rewrite the story to our liking.

The chart that follows will give you the physical attributes for each of the 36 cards; these will be handy when the famous question comes up: "What does she/he look like?"

CARD	NUMBER	ATTRIBUTES
Rider	1	Athletic, fit and slender, strong legs, young
Clover	2	Green eyes, hazel eyes, brown hair
Ship	3	Olive oil skin, tanned skin, robust, exotic
House	4	Square shoulders, well-built, sturdy
Tree	5	Green eyes, tall, healthy

CARD	NUMBER	ATTRIBUTES
Clouds	6	Gray hair, two-toned-colored hair, blue or gray eyes
Snake	7	Tall, slim, sexy
Coffin	8	Square/angular jawline, black hair, dark-colored eyes
Bouquet	9	Good-looking, blond, light-brown, beautiful hair, light skin
Scythe	10	Tattoo or a scar, slim, curvy

CARD	NUMBER	ATTRIBUTES
Whip	11	Fit, sex appeal, strong voice, muscular
Birds	12	Small eyes, piercing voice, distinctive nose
Child	13	Innocent look, young-looking, short/petite
Fox	14	Red/copper hair, elegant walk, slim
Bear	15	Heavy, hairy, voluptuous

CARD	NUMBER	ATTRIBUTES
Stars	16	Flawless skin, birth/beauty mark, attractive eyes
Stork	17	Long legs, tall, slender
Dog	18	Chestnut-brown hair, brown eyes, prominent tongue
Tower	19	Tall, flat-chested, gray hair
Garden	20	Elegant, attractive, good-looking

CARD	NUMBER	ATTRIBUTES
Mountain	21	Large-headed, imposing, gray
Crossroads	22	Hair highlights, two-colored, métisse/Creole
Mice	23	Thin hair, small/petite, rat-faced, small teeth
Heart	24	Cherub face, puffy cheekbones, lovely face
Ring	25	Round, light color

CARD	NUMBER	ATTRIBUTES
Book	26	Wearing glasses, geek, contact lenses
Letter	27	Thin, slim, flat
Lilies	30	Mature face, sexy and attractive, Caucasian, European origin
Sun	31	Blond, fair skin, blue eyes
Moon	32	Pale, porcelain skin, round face, glamorous

CARD	NUMBER	ATTRIBUTES
Key	33	Skinny, strong, nor too tall nor to small
Fish	34	Dark hair and skin, Mediterranean look, green or blue eyes
Anchor	35	Curve, large hips, tanned skin, colored eyes
Cross	36	Long arms/long legs, exhausted look, straight posture

PLAYING CARD
INSERTS

The Lenormand deck is derived from the Piquet deck, which is a playing card deck of 32 cards, 7–10 plus the court cards, this is the reason why each Lenormand card has a playing card insert. These inserts can be used in a reading; the court cards can represent people in your life; the suits (hearts, diamonds, spades, and clubs), numbers. This information can be useful, for example, when you want to know the gender of an expected baby.

The chart that follows provides cartomantic meanings for each card, based upon the French cartomancy system.

HEARTS

The heart suit is about love, romance, good and true
feelings, family, and everything that you cherish.

DIAMONDS

The diamond suit is about the evolution of your project,
about the action that needs to be taken.

CLUBS

The clubs are about business, whether associative or
professional. It also covers work and your relationship
with money.

SPADES

The spades are about obstacles and difficulties, similar
to the swords in the Tarot.

HEARTS

CARD	NUMBER	PLAYING CARD	CARTOMANTIC MEANING
Man	28	ACE	Personal life, joy, pleasure, falling in love, the home
House	4	KING	A protector, a good man, devoted person, male querent
Stork	17	QUEEN	Beloved, a mother, fair skin, female querent
Heart	24	JACK	Young blond man, idealistic, great sensitivity, a lover, a fiancé, a brother

CARD	NUMBER	PLAYING CARD	CARTOMANTIC MEANING
Dog	18	10	Positive issue, an invitation, a celebration
Rider	1	9	Positive outcome, a victory, a wish come true
Moon	32	8	A young girl, sensitive person, a good heart, a sister
Tree	5	7	Tranquility, positive feelings, can sometimes represent a child
Stars	16	6	The memories, hope

DIAMONDS

CARD	NUMBER	PLAYING CARD	CARTOMANTIC MEANING
Sun	31	ACE	News, information, letter, contract
Fish	34	KING	A businessman, a foreigner, ambitious man, ex-husband
Crossroads	22	QUEEN	Jealousy, a rival, a warning, a foreigner, gossip, ex-wife
Scythe	10	JACK	Message bearer, news, decision, an ex-lover

CARD	NUMBER	PLAYING CARD	CARTOMANTIC MEANING
Book	26	10	Travel, change, movement, relocation
Coffin	8	9	Blockage, delays, standstill
Key	33	8	A confirmation, a target, a goal
Birds	12	7	Projects, plans, transaction
Clover	2	6	Reward, small gift, surprise

CLUBS

CARD	NUMBER	PLAYING CARD	CARTOMANTIC MEANING
Ring	25	ACE	Triumph, great success, alliance
Clouds	6	KING	A mature man, close to his money, an uncle
Snake	7	QUEEN	A mature woman, close to her money, an aunt
Whip	11	JACK	Young man, attracted by money, nephew, cousin

CARD	NUMBER	PLAYING CARD	CARTOMANTIC MEANING
Bear	15	10	Abundance, prosperity, large sum of money
Fox	14	9	Your work, your day job, what pays the bill
Mountain	21	8	A brunette, small sum of money, nephew, cousin
Mice	23	7	Thoughts, your hope, your expectations
Cross	36	6	Obstacles, pain, difficulties

SPADES

CARD	NUMBER	PLAYING CARD	CARTOMANTIC MEANING
Woman	29	ACE	An opening, legal papers, separation
Lilies	30	KING	A widower, divorced man, mature man, grandfather
Bouquet	9	QUEEN	A widow, divorced woman, mature woman, grandmother
Child	13	JACK	Warning, betrayal, childish, a traitor

CARD	NUMBER	PLAYING CARD	CARTOMANTIC MEANING
Ship	3	10	Very quick, doubts, by night
Anchor	35	9	Unexpected event, fatality, danger
Garden	20	8	Feeling tired, drained, exhausted, health issue
Letter	27	7	Certifies an event, favorable event, for sure, a yes answer
Tower	19	6	Argument, discussion, small trouble

QUARTETS AND PAIRS, TRIPLETS

In Lenormand, a combination gives extra information in a reading; so too does the meeting of multiple playing cards. In the following chart you will find keywords that will help you memorize the meanings of the quartets, triplets, and pairs. I chose to display Spades here, bun any of the suits are appropriate.

PLAYING CARD	PAIR	TRIPLET	QUARTET
ACE	Success	Prosperity	Triumph
KING	An opening	Guided	Protection
QUEEN	Affinity	Rivalry	Jealousy
JACK	Warning	Arguments	Discussion

PLAYING CARD	PAIR	TRIPLET	QUARTET
10 10♠	Small change	Movement	Transformation
9 9♠	Hard work	Continue the good work	Harvesting, reward
8 8♠	Feelings	Engagement	Wedding
7 7♠	Doubts	Pregnancy	Birth
6 6♠	Compassion	Serenity	Harmony

LENORMAND
CARD SPREADS

The layout of cards in a pattern is called a card spread. Each position in the spread has a meaning, and there are many different types of spreads, ranging from those that incorporate 2 cards to spreads that include all 36 Lenormand cards. In this section of the book, I will explain card spreads and how to use them. We will start with the basic and fundamental ones which are the 3-, 5-, 7-, and 9-card spreads that leads to the gigantic Grand Tableau.

STRING OR A RUN (OF CARDS)

The 3-, 5-, and 7-card spreads are also known as "string." This is where you lay out the cards from left to right in a horizontal line. These strings are usually used to answer one question at a time.

Before we jump into the card layout I want to specify that a spread has different goals, and it is the intention of the reader who makes the spread speak out clearly and loudly. As there are different kinds of spreads, there are many ways of reading them; let me explain.

NARRATIVE TECHNIQUE

The Lenormand is read like a book, readers often refer to it as a narrative technique of interpretation, going from the first card, which is the point of focus, to the last one, narrating the story of the querent's concern.

FOCUS CARD

In this method, the center card is the focus; it talks about the current situation; the other cards describe it further and add additional information to the answer or situation.

CHARGED OR ACTIVATED CARD

In this technique, we choose a Significator in your spread—for instance, Heart 24 for love, Fox 14 for work, Fish 34 for money (check out the chapter on Significators). As you shuffle, speak out your question and think of the card that will represent the question; when you feel you're done with shuffling, go through the deck till you find your Significator/activated card. Pay extra attention to the cards that sandwich the Significator/activated card, and take the one before and the one after the Significator/activated. Now you have a

3-card spread: the charged card becomes the focus, and the other 2 cards describe the situation. For a 5-7-card read, just pull enough before and after to get your desired amount of cards for the spread.

PAST, PRESENT, FUTURE

This is a technique similar to the focus card, where the center card is the current situation, the cards before it are the past influence and the cards after the focus card are the future dynamic.

Always tell the cards what you want them to do, and they will work upon your request to give you the best true answer.

3-CARD SPREAD

The 3-card spread is an easy and fast way to get a clear answer. The center card is always the focus; it represents the situation. The cards on the side describe it, and I see the last card as the answer or the punctuation to the reading.

Let's look at an example reading. Marie has a question regarding her love life; she wants to know if Marc will propose to her. After shuffling, I lay down 3 cards as shown below:

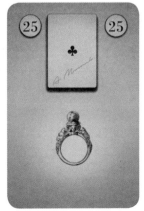

STORK 17 + HEART 24 + RING 25

The focus card is the Heart in the center, and we see that they truly love each other. The Stork on the left predicts a positive change, and the Ring tells us that without a doubt Marc will propose to her. The 3-card spread can be used for a "yes and no" question by simply counting the number of positive and negative cards. More of positive cards = "yes." More negative = "no." I describe another "yes or no" method later in the book.

Master the 3-card spread before moving to more complex ones; this will help you increase your accuracy and build your self-confidence in Lenormand reading. The 3-card spread is the most basic, and its principles apply to larger spreads.

5-CARD SPREAD

"RAISE YOUR WORDS NOT YOUR VOICE."
—RUMI

The 5-card spread is as quick and easy as the 3-card spread, with more detail. The center card is still the focus card, and the 4 others describe the situation. Everything to the left refers to the past or to current events, and everything to the right is what is to become or the future. I like to see this spread as a snapshot where a situation can be seen under a new light.

Marc wants to know about his career; he really wants to know if he will get a promotion and how can he achieve it quickly.

Here are the cards that come up:

RIDER 1, CLOVER 2, HOUSE 4, SNAKE 7, AND COFFIN 8

We see that the focus card is the House, showing that Marc must leave his comfort zone and move his butt to gain new opportunity (Rider + Clover) for his company. He needs to show that he can turn (or manipulate) the situation to his advantage (Snake). The Coffin tells us that no promotion will be given as long as Marc remains stagnant. As you see, you can give a clear reading in no time with Lenormand; the cards get right to the essential points.

7-CARD SPREAD

The 7-card spread is interesting, as it is the combination of 2 pairs of triplet card sets on either side of the focus card. Beginning from the left, the first grouping of 3 provides information about the recent past—what the client has been experiencing. The middle card is the focus of what is happening in the present, and the grouping of 3 cards on the right tell of the outcome, advice, solution, or result. Let's see how it works in a reading.

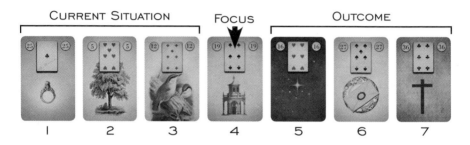

Stephan wants to know if he will be traveling in June. I shuffle the cards and randomly pull 7 cards and place them in a horizontal line (see the string above). The focus card here is the Tower 19, and it gives me the feeling that Stephen had already planned and structured this trip and that this trip may involve legal matters. From the recent past, the Ring 25, Tree 5, Birds 12 show that Stephen has been thinking of the travel details, planning a short trip (Birds); the Ring and Tree show that there is some kind of legacy or inheritance involved, perhaps the reason for this trip. With the Tower, the idea of legal matters concerning inheritance becomes stronger. The outcome cards are Stars 16, Letter 27, Cross 36; Stephen hopes to travel (Stars), but some kind of burden will be blocking the trip (Cross) related to a document, messages, or booking (Letter).

My answer to Stephen was that he would not be able to travel due to some paper issues, and maybe he could sort out what the problem is and change the course of this outcome. After the reading, Stephen told me that the purpose of his travel regarded legal matters that needed to be resolved because of the passing of his dad, and that he was actually waiting for a reply from the attorney before buying his tickets. Lenormand was right, and the line of 7 has once again shown everything clearly!

9-CARD SPREAD/ BOX SPREAD/ SQUARE OF 9

The 9-card "Box Spread" is one of my favorites; I use it often in my private practice, and you can see my YouTube videos where I give readings using this spread. It provides so much information from the cards and their interactions. There are many ways to lay down and interpret the "Box Spread"; below is a schema to guide you in the way I lay down and interpret the cards.

MEANING OF THE POSITIONS

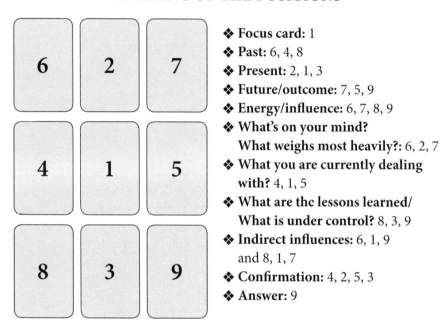

❖ **Focus card:** 1
❖ **Past:** 6, 4, 8
❖ **Present:** 2, 1, 3
❖ **Future/outcome:** 7, 5, 9
❖ **Energy/influence:** 6, 7, 8, 9
❖ **What's on your mind?**
  What weighs most heavily?: 6, 2, 7
❖ **What you are currently dealing**
  with? 4, 1, 5
❖ **What are the lessons learned/**
  What is under control? 8, 3, 9
❖ **Indirect influences:** 6, 1, 9
  and 8, 1, 7
❖ **Confirmation:** 4, 2, 5, 3
❖ **Answer:** 9

You will use the 9-card spread a lot in interpreting a Grand Tableau reading. So I recommend getting comfortable using it. Each time that you want to know about an area of your life in The Grand Tableau, you will box the Significator and align to the situation; for instance, when you would like to see about your health, you can box the Tree 5, and this card then becomes card 1, the focus card in the box spread. I explain this in the following sections on The Grand Tableau reading.

THE GRAND TABLEAU

THE GRAND TABLEAU

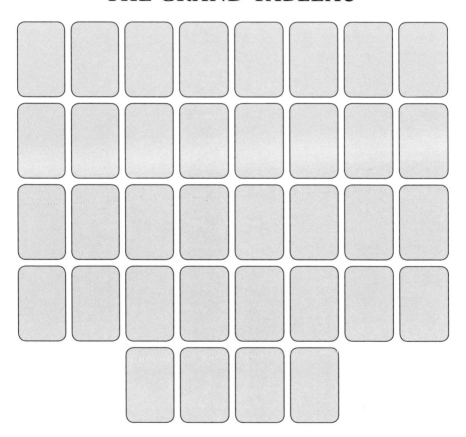

So you see, everything leads to The Grand Tableau! The Grand Tableau (GT) is a French term that means "Big Picture," and is a unique system of divination that uses all 36 cards of the Lenormand deck at once. I consider The Grand Tableau as a magical map of life that holds a richness of guidance and power.

When I open the cards, the GT reveals my client's journey, telling where he came from, what landscape he is experiencing at this very moment, and what is about to come to him. The GT can bring to light hidden influences and patterns that may be blocking him from progressing or accomplishing what he wants.

With the GT, he can see what's happening in his love life, finances, career, health, friendships, spirituality, family—in short, everything that concerns his life.

Note: I use an 8 × 4 + 4 formation in my GT readings, rather than a 9 × 5

Everything that you've been reading from the previous chapters will be used in a GT. To simplify learning and mastering such a large reading, I will section The Grand Tableau into 8 keys that you can utilize to read your GT successfully. When I cast a Grand Tableau, I ask my clients to cut the cards and focus on what they would like to know. Remember that the GT can reply to several questions at once and also give a sneak peek of any other area of life. I will use diagrams to help me in my explanation. I have found that visual examples of the patterns leave a favorable imprint in one's mind, and make things easier to remember.

Shuffle your cards and deal them in an [8 × 4] + 4 formation, with the cards faceup.

The GT is for advanced readers; if you are a newbie to Lenormand, please don't start with the GT right away. You will need to get the fundamentals first, master the card meanings, the small spreads, and get to know your cards, as all of this work and training will build and help you immensely in your GT. If you start right from the GT, you will find the system overwhelming and will be discouraged, perhaps thinking that Lenormand is not for you. In truth, Lenormand is for everyone who wants to invest time and discipline into learning and playing with it.

Keep it fun, and let's begin our exploration!

8 KEYS TO READING
THE GRAND TABLEAU

"YOU SUPPOSE THAT YOU ARE THE LOCK ON THE DOOR,
BUT YOU ARE THE KEY THAT OPENS IT."
—RUMI

KEY 1

The First 3 Cards of The Tableau

These 3 cards open the game and set the theme and the tone of the reading. They will talk about what is being brought to the table.

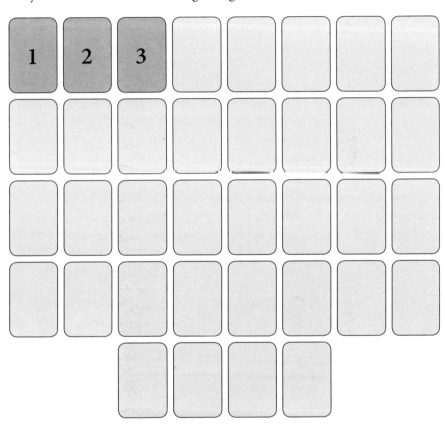

At this point in your practice, you've perhaps been mastering the 3-card reading, and here it comes in play. For instance:

BOUQUET 9, MOON 32 + STARS 16

We will be talking about the dreams and wishes the querent has, and his/her aspirations. The reading starts on a positive note.

Remember to align the meaning of the cards with the context of the question so that the meaning can perfectly match the situation. The Grand Tableau is a collection of small spreads that lead to the Grand reading.

Let's move to the next step.

KEY 2
Where the Significator Lands

Notice where your Significator Man 28 or Woman 29 landed on The Tableau. Everything that lies at the left is his past; everything to his right is the future, and everything in the line on top and bottom of him is his present.

Their position in The Tableau gives valuable clues: If they are on the top row, this will indicate that they have control over the situation and know how to deal with things. If they fall to the bottom row, this indicates that they have weight on their shoulders; the whole Tableau is on them! Oftentimes this is a sign that the querent is overwhelmed, and has lost control with the course of events.

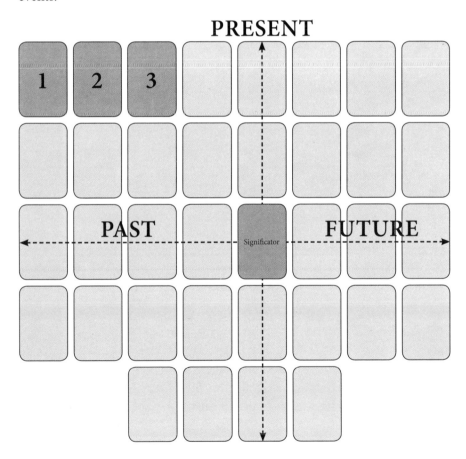

When the Significator happens to be in the first row on the left, this tells me that she/he is starting a new chapter in life and can look forward to an eventful future. Inversely, if the Significator card lands on the last row on the right, this tells me that there is an upcoming end of a chapter, and she/he may be still attached to the past.

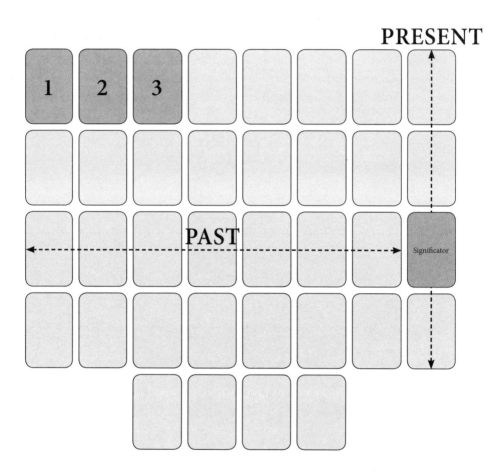

Many readers get panicked when there seems to be no future cards showing; some will want to reshuffle the cards or use another divination system to see the future. For my part, I never re-deal the cards. If the GT has appeared this way, it is for a reason; it is simply that a lesson needs to be learned before the future can happen.

KEY 3

The Four Corners

I use the four corners of The Tableau to see what the energy is, in action, the dynamics. Oftentimes these areas show things that the querent is not aware of. These can be elements that frame the situation; view them as pieces of tape, holding the corners of a poster or a large calendar on the wall.

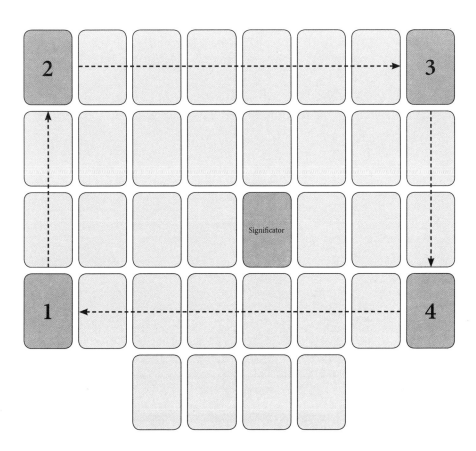

Some examples include the following:

ANCHOR 35 + MOUNTAIN 21 + CLOUDS 6 + CROSS 36
Indicates a blockage; maybe the energy needs to be cleared so that the desired outcome can happen. Or perhaps an established pattern needs to be cleared up.

BOUQUET 9 + MOON 32 + KEY 33 + DOG 18
Indicates that a trusted friend is providing help and hope to the querent, or that success is coming through a good friend in a surprising way.

SCYTHE 10, WHIP 11 + CROSS 36 + COFFIN 8
Indicates an ending or separation; something is falling apart.

KEY 4
Near and Far: The Distance
(My Method)

This method uses the proximity of certain cards to determine their direct impact on the game. They will have different meanings if they are near to or far from the Significator card: Man 28, Woman 29.

There are 7 cards that I take a close look at when reading the GT, as they provide significant information with their distance. Of course this is my personal take on that method; the distance technique is more of the German Lenormand school.

Card 4: The House

If the house appears in the center of The Tableau, it is a warning to be on your guard; the surrounding cards will tell you about the danger.

Card 5: Tree

If far from the Significator, the Tree denotes good health; closeness to the person shows health issues.

Card 25: Ring

On the right-hand side of the Significator, the Ring predicts a strong and happy partnership/marriage. On the left-hand side of the Significator, it predicts separation and unhappy partnership.

Card 30: Lilies

On top of the Significator, Lilies announces a trustworthy, loyal person. Below the Significator, it announces dishonesty and worries.

Card 31: Sun

Close to the Significator, the Sun indicates success, happiness, and good outcome; when far, it indicates anxiety, failure, and worries.

Card 32: Moon

Close to the Significator, the Moon indicates hope, clarity, and acknowledgment; when far, it is a sign of disillusion.

Card 35: Anchor

Close to the Significator, the Anchor is a sign of prosperity, of goals fulfilled; when far, it announces a disappointment.

KEY 5

Box the Significator

This is where the 9-card spread or box spread becomes handy. You will box the Significator and read the spread, as explained previously in the chapter about the reading smaller card spreads.

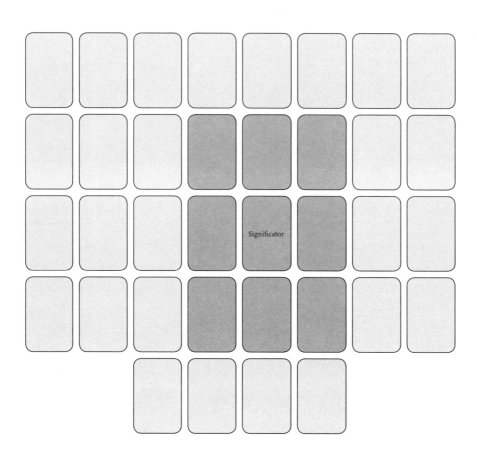

KEY 6

The Lenormand Houses

House 1	House 2	House 3	House 4	House 5	House 6	House 7	House 8
Rider	**Clover**	**Ship**	**House**	**Tree**	**Clouds**	**Snake**	**Coffin**
—	—	—	—	—	—	—	—
News Movement	Opportunity Luck	Travel Change	Family Property	Health Growth	Confusion Doubts	Lies Betrayals	Ending Change

House 9	House 10	House 11	House 12	House 13	House 14	House 15	House 16
Bouquet	**Scythe**	**Whip**	**Birds**	**Child**	**Fox**	**Bear**	**Stars**
—	—	—	—	—	—	—	—
Happiness Beauty	Danger Ending	Conflict Repetition	Talks Couple	New Innocence	Work Trickery	Finances Strength	Dream Ambition

House 17	House 18	House 19	House 20	House 21	House 22	House 23	House 24
Stork	**Dog**	**Tower**	**Garden**	**Mountain**	**Crossroads**	**Mice**	**Heart**
—	—	—	—	—	—	—	—
A move Upgrade	Friendship Third party	Structure Hierarchy	Networking Group	Blocks Obstacles	Choice Decisions	Loss Stress	Love Romance

House 25	House 26	House 27	House 28	House 29	House 30	House 31	House 32
Ring	**Book**	**Letter**	**Man**	**Woman**	**Lilies**	**Sun**	**Moon**
—	—	—	—	—	—	—	—
Love Romance	Secrets Plans	Written Communication	Male Querent	Female Querent	Maturity Loyalty	Success Great luck	Intuition Recognition

House 33	House 34	House 35	House 36
Key	**Fish**	**Anchor**	**Cross**
—	—	—	—
Solution Importance	Transaction Abundance	Stability Goals	Burdens Trials

What are the Lenormand houses? The Lenormand houses are all of the 36 cards of the deck, laid out in numerical order 1–36, in a (8 × 4) + 4 formation.

The houses are stagnant and never change, and each card that falls on them are colored by the energy of that house. For example, the Bouquet 9 in the house of the Rider 1 announces surprising positive news, or that someone will receive a gift. I tend to see the houses as the space a card occupies: the Man 28 falling on house of the Book 26 would mean that the querent is busy with studies, whereas the Woman 29 falling on the house of the House 4 would be busy with domestic chores.

Let say the Ring 25 is on the house of the Woman 29, this will indicate that the female querent is in a serious partnership, or engaged. The house-matching technique does add more dimension to the reading of The Grand Tableau. Pay attention to which house your Significator falls on; this is precious information and can add good detail to your reading. When a card falls on its own house, the meaning is stronger: for instance, Mountain 21, in the house of the Mountain would mean a strong blockage, a mighty enemy.

The Snake in the house of the Snake: Beware, you are exploring a dangerous landscape.

KEY 7
Knighting

The Knighting method gives additional information on a card. The name regards a move similar to the one in a chess game. The knight on the chessboard moves outward from its position in a perpendicular movement (L-shaped move). The original card of departure is then combined with the knighted cards. Here is a diagram to help you visualize the move.

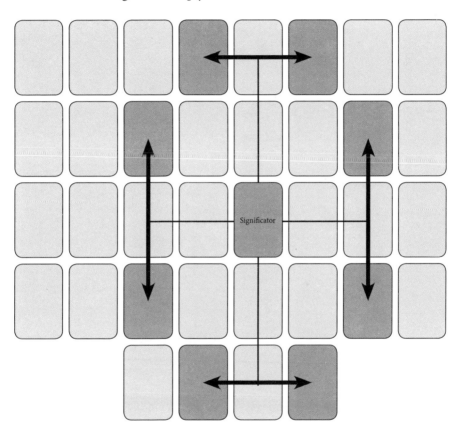

The Knighting method can be used on any card. For example, concerning the family, knight the House 4; for a partnership, knight the Ring 25; knight the Bear 15 for money. Depending on the position of your Significator in The Tableau, you can get 2–8 knighted cards. (From the card of departure, count 2 on top and 1 left of right, creating a reversed L.)

KEY 8

The Line of Wisdom

The Line of Wisdom are the last four cards of The Tableau, the bottom row. These serve as the punctuation to your reading or, as I read, a message that the Divine would like you to know. It can also be used to answer a precise question. (For this, you must tell the cards before you begin laying cards down that the last 4 cards will answer this particular question.)

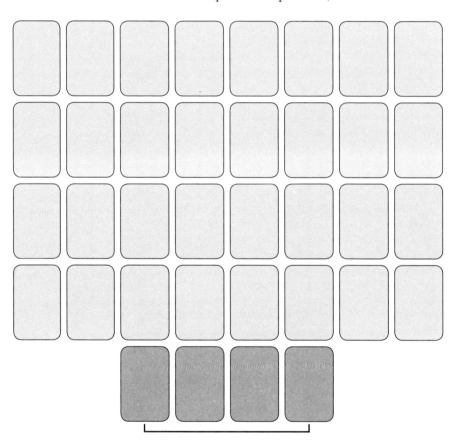

A REAL READING
USING THE GRAND
TABLEAU

"WEAR GRATITUDE LIKE A CLOAK,
AND IT WILL FEED EVERY CORNER OF YOUR LIFE."
—RUMI

This next Grand Tableau is a real client reading. Sarah came to me because she had some issues with her work. She works in the medical and health care industry; her boss is someone quite difficult to deal with who sees her own interests first over those of the team. When the department was sold to a corporation, they changed their working hours. At first Sarah and her colleagues were stressed, and then finally adapted themselves to the new change. A year and a half later, the boss announced that the corporation wanted to restore the old working hours for the benefit of all. Sarah was worried, as she had changed her family/home/chores/work timetable due to the new working hours, and now she would have to make more new changes. She wanted the cards to answer the following questions:

❖ Will they change the working hours?

❖ What will the ambience at work be like?

❖ What are the real motives of the boss? (As she was the one asking for the first change, and now is the one asking to change things back to the original hours.)

❖ What is the point of view of the corporation?

❖ Can any additional advice be provided?

At first glance this seems a lot to answer in a reading, but this is the beauty of the Lenormand and The Grand Tableau! With practice, The Grand Tableau can answer many questions at once. As I shuffle my cards, I ask Sarah to think and speak her questions aloud while she cuts the deck.

I always let my client touch my cards; I want them to infuse their question into the cards and be involved in the process. I want (as clearly as possible) to know what message the cards are being asked to convey.

In the last chapter I will share with you my method of clearing and charging my cards; this will ensure clarity of your readings, and you will no longer have to be afraid to let people touch your cards, because you will have a sound method by which to cleanse and clear them between client readings.

For Sarah, I activated 4 cards for this reading: the Bear 15, representing the boss, the Tower 19, representing the corporation, the Fox 14, representing Sarah's work and workplace; and the Ring 25. The Ring 25 will answer Sarah's first question: Will they change the working hours? (See the method in the additional spread section on page 186.)

Here is Sarah's Grand Tableau; follow along as I translate the messages of The Grand Tableau for Sarah.

Will They Change the Working Hours?

We begin with the first three cards of the GT; remember these cards give the first notes to the reading—they show what focus is brought to the table. We have the Rider 1 + Ring 25 + Child 13. This combination of cards tells me that news of a new commitment is announced; the Rider in his own house reinforces that news is on its way.

The cards reflect exactly what Sarah is experiencing, validate her concerns, and at the same time answer her first question (Will they change the working hours?) with a "yes," as the ring is in the first 13 cards of the draw. (I explain in the chapter called "More Card Spreads" how the Ring is used in a "yes or no" question.)

Now let's look at the four corners. Here we get Woman 29 + Rider 1 + Coffin 8 + Heart 24. The energy is directly impacting Sarah, as she is part of the corner cards.

The cards clearly show that Sarah wants things to end (Woman + Coffin) and that a happy change can occur (Rider + Heart).

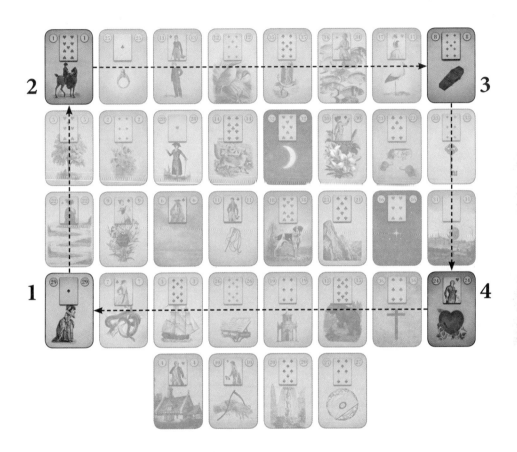

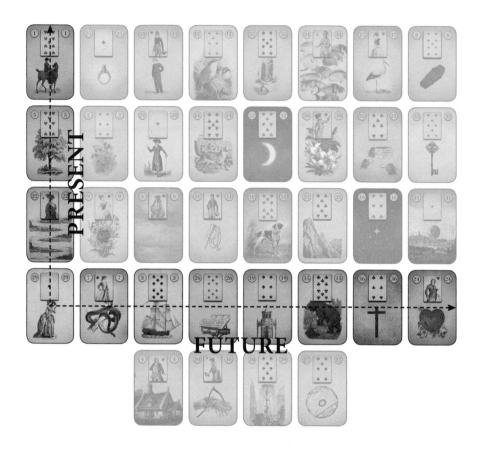

The Woman 29 card is in the first row, indicating that she is starting a new phase in her life, and being under The Tableau denotes how overwhelmed and stressed she is about the situation. The way The Tableau appears gives no place for "a past" column, and this is an indication that Sarah is more focused on her future.

PRESENT LINE: CROSSROADS 22 + TREE 5 + RIDER 1

These cards tell us that Sarah is at a crossroads, facing serious doubts with her work. The tree can signify health issues related to the present situation. The Rider is strongly present in her current situation, and the Rider represents the news she is longing to know.

FUTURE LINE: SNAKE 7 + SHIP 3 + BOOK 26 + TOWER 19 + BEAR 15 + CROSS 36 + HEART 24

This is a very interesting line, as it reveals the future and the unfolding of events. The Snake shows that she will be facing an enemy. A Woman and Bear on the same line tells me that she will face her boss who keeps a secret (Book) with or for the corporation (Tower). The boss herself is a burden (Bear + Cross) and will make Sarah's heart heavy. I get the sense that Sarah's boss has used manipulation to get what she wants—the cards clearly show her motives to have more freedom (Ship).

Now, with the Near and Far Method that I explained before, I look for my 7 key cards of distance.

All of the key cards I use in the Near and Far Method are far away from Sarah (Woman), except for the Tree 5, a sign of health issues related to her work. (She confirmed that she had heavy migraines since the whole issue started.)

The querent can't be boxed in a 9-card spread, as there are not enough cards around her to use. Let us proceed to the Houses Method.

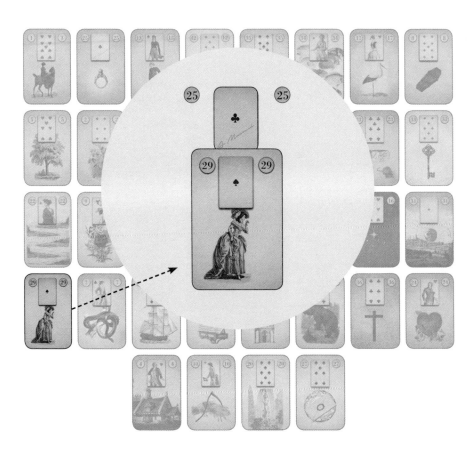

Sarah is in house 25, house of the Ring, the house of commitment, showing that she wants to know if the commitment they had will still continue. And being in this house is also telling me she wants things to continue the same way (Ring = circle = continuation).

Her Line of Wisdom represents advice—what Sarah can do to help her situation. She drew House 4 + Scythe 10 + Garden 20 + Letter 27 indicating that Sarah and her coworkers should leave their comfort zone and speak of their dismay to the corporate powers that be through written correspondence.

This should be a letter that her boss should not know about, as she has the power to conceal it (Bear on Letter) and block the information.

What Will the Ambience at Work Be Like?

To answer this question, I use the Fox 14, which I have activated to represent the work and workplace of Sarah. We note here that the Fox is in the house of the Birds 12, the house of conversation and gossip.

We can conclude that there are a lot of rumors going around. The top line stands for what is on Sarah's mind—Child 13 + Birds 12 + Anchor 35—indicating that she and all the employees' minds are filled with persistent rumors about their workplace, not knowing what is really going on. I surmised that they are actually dealing with someone who is deceptive, not showing their motives and true aspirations to the group, Man 28 + Fox 14 + Moon 32. What they know for sure is that someone, a third party, is provoking the turmoil, Clouds 6 + Whip 11 + Dog 18. The third party involved in this story is clearly shown again with Child 13 + Fox 14 +Dog 18, someone who plays an innocent game and pretends to be a good and trustworthy friend, someone in the workplace itself, Clouds 6 + Fox 14 + Anchor 35.

The Dog at the end of the box assures that friendship will be the answer; as long as these employees stay united, they can make things change. Another confirmation of this is shown by the Line of Wisdom.

What Is the Point of View of the Corporation?

Here I will use the Knighting Method; remember, I activated the Tower card as the Significator for the corporate powers that be, or her Sarah's bosses.

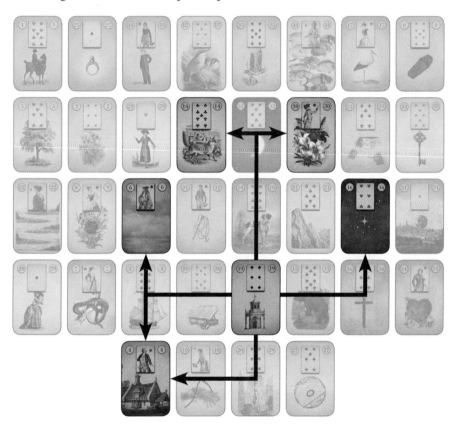

TOWER 19 + FOX 14 + LILIES 30:
A conspiracy at work

TOWER 19 + HOUSE 4 + CLOUDS 6:
A confused workplace

TOWER 19 + STARS 16:
A well-known industry

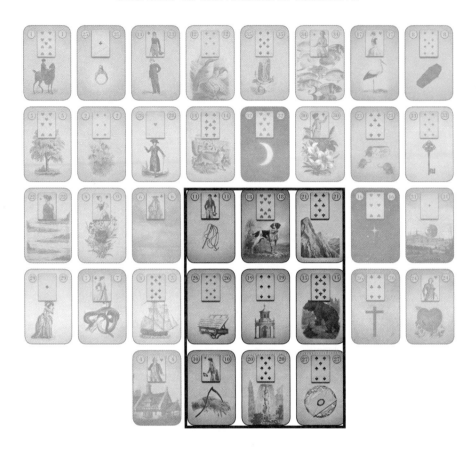

The Knighting Method shows that the corporation is not aware of the impact of the change on the workers' schedules, and the employees need to inform them. Let us box the Tower to understand this point.

WHIP 11 + DOG 18 + MOUNTAIN 21:
Shows a disagreement, an enemy getting in between one's friends.

BOOK 26 + TOWER 19 + BEAR 15:
A revelation made to both the corporation and the boss.

SCYTHE 10+ GARDEN 20 + LETTER 27:
Cutting through with an email, asking for a meeting.

The solution for sure is the Letter, which stands for communicating, dialoguing, and informing. My conclusion is that the boss is manipulating everybody, including the higher corporate bosses and the workers. She wants more freedom, sees her interests first, and wants everybody to obey her. My guess is that the corporation has no idea of what is going on and thinks that everybody agrees and that they are happy to modify their working hours again. Sarah and her coworkers need to write to the corporate higher-ups, clearly explaining their dismay and their confusion about the changes and utter lack of communication. As long as the team stays united, they can work wonders.

After the reading, Sarah was happy; the reading shed light on what was going on, and she decided to organize a meeting with her coworkers. They gladly accepted and agreed to sign a petition that would present their disagreement concerning the changes. Discreetly, everything was sent on to the corporate bosses. For the outcome, I will let Sarah tell you of the results.

Dear Alexandre,

I must thank you for the reading that brought so much clarity and was of great help to guide me in this situation. We've just finished the meeting with the corporation, and they clearly affirm that they were not aware of the turmoil created by the change of working hours. They apologized and decided that the working hours will not be changed and that for future decisions they will directly talk to the employees. As you may know, our boss is furious about the decision, but it doesn't matter at all; we are now working peacefully again and we thank you for that...

Sarah

MORE CARD SPREADS

YES OR NO

This is a reading method I've been using for decades with playing cards. The system comes from French cartomancy and is called *La réussite*, meaning "a success or triumph." In cartomancy, the Aces are the most powerful cards in the game; they announce significant positive events. This method is used via a Piquet deck. A 32-card deck, 7–10 plus the court cards are shuffled. The first 13 cards are drawn from the top of the deck and flipped over. If the Ace of Clubs, "*As de trèfle,*" is in the run of cards, it announces a success and a "yes" answer. If the Ace of Clubs is not there, your answer is "no."

You can use the same technique with Lenormand; we will use the Ring 25 as its card insert is the Ace of Clubs.

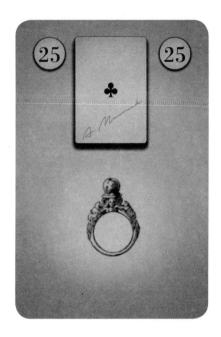

Shuffle the cards, and when you feel ready, flip over the first 13 cards from the top of the deck. If the Ring card is part of the draw, the answer is "yes," and if the Ring is absent, the answer is "no."

If the answer is "no," you can actually look for what may be blocking your success. Look for the Ring card in the deck, and take the cards that surround it, one before and one after, and interpret these cards.

THE CROSS SPREAD

This is a spread that I like to use to analyze a situation; it gives clues as to what is going on, as well as where one's weaknesses and strengths lie. You don't need to have a precise question to use this spread. You can use a single card for each position, but I like to use 3 cards each, as it gives even more valuable information. You will read the 3 cards the same way you've seen in the previous chapters. Here is the placement and their meaning:

1. Where you are at now

2. What is out of your reach

3. What you already have

4. What you should surrender

5. What you are bringing into your life

THE CROSS IN ACTION

Claire wants to know about her love life—if there is someone for her out there, and any useful advice that she can use to attract a potential partner.

I shuffle the cards and focus on Claire's love life. I invite her to cut the cards, and I deal the cards in the Cross in Action spread.

Position 1: Where you are at now
Garden 20, Ring 25, Snake 7

We see here that Claire is focused on a committed relationship. She is not looking for love with a big L but for a partner. The Garden tells me that she has an eye on someone in her social circle, a seductive and dangerous person.

Position 2: What is out of your reach
Whip 11, Heart 24, Tree 5

The Heart being out of Claire's reach confirms that she has no lover at this time, only sex stories, nothing serious at all, and no one wants to be in a relationship with her (Heart + Tree).

Position 3: What you already have
Bear 15, Clouds 6, Birds 12

Lots of confusion is going on here; the cards give me the sense that with the Bear and the Birds, the way that she talks and expresses herself may be seen as rude (which could discourage a potential partner). This can be a behavior that makes any potential partner run.

Position 4: What you should surrender
Man 28, Scythe 10, Rider 1

Here's the man Claire has her eyes on. The cards are advising her to cut away her intentions with him. The presence of the Scythe is significant here; the Rider adds movement, meaning that this man will not stay. Why waste time with him?

Position 5: What you are bringing into your life
Cross 36, Dog 18, House 4

The Cross tells me that there is a pattern here; people she attracts may treat her badly and abuse her. She needs to do some work on her self-esteem and raise her standards. As the cards have shown before, she must change the way she expresses herself. In the French Lenormand system, when the Dog 18 is near the House 4 surrounded by negative cards, the Dog becomes a traitor.

MY SIGNATURE SPREAD
DOUBLE LINE OF 7

Through my many years of reading the Lenormand, I have made a spread of my own that has become my signature spread. This is a great technique if you want to give a detailed reading on a particular concern. The top row of seven cards will represent the houses, and the bottom row will be the cards.

In this spread, you can apply the precious techniques of pairing, mirroring, and knighting. It is not as big as The Grand Tableau, but a nice chunk of information. As shown in the diagram, you can read the focus, current situation, and outcome by reading the house and cards (as previously instructed).

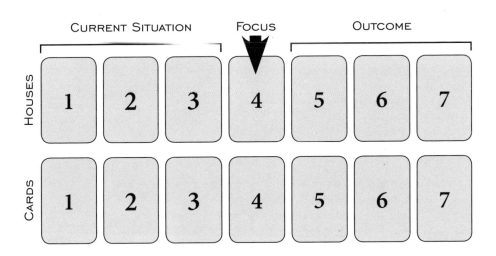

ATTUNE YOUR DECK
OF LENORMAND
FOR DIVINATION

"Be melting snow; wash
yourself with yourself."
—Rumi

CLEARING YOUR LENORMAND DECK

Oracle cards are sensitive, as they absorb surrounding energies. This is why you need to clear them before each reading you conduct. Clearing the cards on a regular basis is essential, as you don't want the energies of the previous person you've read for to influence the next reading. Not only do the cards need to be cleared, but the box, pouch, or any item you house your deck in needs to be purified also. When you clear the deck, you bring it back to its neutral state. There are many ways of clearing your cards—all are effective, but not all will work for you. I will explain my technique; hopefully this will inspire you to find and create your own clearing ritual. Choose one that feels right and suits your needs and beliefs.

SETTING YOUR INTENTION THROUGH PRAYER

Always tell the cards what you would like them to do for you!

They are your best friend; they listen and hear you, and the wisdom they convey is unlimited—you just need to ask. I believe in the power of prayer. Prayer for me doesn't belong to any one religion and does not have any structured way about it. For me prayer is a heart-to-heart conversation with the Most High Creator or Spirit Guides, and you can ask whatever help you would like through your cards in your reading. When I clear my cards I often say:

> Dear God and all of my Spirit Guides, I ask that everything that is not from your Divine light be lifted away now from these cards. Thank you.

I also use crystals to clear my cards. The crystals I use are angelite, lapis lazuli, celestite, selenite, and clear crystal quartz. I simply place one crystal on top of my cards and let them sit for a few hours. Smudging your cards with incense or white sage is also a good way to clear your Lenormand deck; the smoke will banish any old energy from your cards and leave them fresh and clear.

BLESSING YOUR CARDS

I also use a prayer to bless my cards; I will speak an invocation as I hold them in my hands:

> Dear God and Spirit Guides, I ask that these cards become sacred tools for divine guidance and be a blessing for myself, my clients, and everyone involved. Help me stay centered so I may easily understand the messages that the cards want to convey. Thank you.

You can light a white candle next to your cards as a sign of blessing or expose them to moonlight. There are various ways you can bless your cards, and I always choose the simplest and shortest methods—I find them to be more effective.

From the *Creole Lenormand* by Alexandre Musruck

ABOUT RUMI

Jalāl ad-Dīn Muhammad Balkhī, also known as Rumi, was a thirteenth-century Persian poet, jurist, theologian, and Sufi mystic who wrote some of the most beautiful and profound words ever recorded. I am grateful for his words of wisdom that inspire me so much. I hope you enjoyed his words throughout this book.

ACKNOWLEDGMENTS

Life can plan things in a weird way; synchronicity creates amazing events: like a young boy just wanting a deck of Tarot cards seen in a James Bond movie, who instead was given a strange little deck of cards from Belgium bearing the name of a strange woman, "Mademoiselle Lenormand."

I want to start by thanking Life and the extraordinary Being (God, Great Spirit, any name you give him) that animates it, who behind the scenes had orchestrated all of these beautiful moments of my life. I was given the mission to help and empower people, I've accepted it with open arms and heart, and my life has never been the same. I want to give thanks to the thousands of people who during these twenty-three years let me "read" the story of their lives—many said that I was a blessing in their life, but in truth, *they* were the blessing. Without them I could not be the "Lenormand Extraordinaire!"

To my ancestors, to those who walked this path before me, I hope that I have honored you and our lineage; thank you for being always around.

To my dear friends and family who understood my gift before even I was aware of it and did not run away; your support and unconditional love mean a lot to me.

To my dear followers on social media, particularly my YouTube subscribers— you are awesome, and sharing this space with you is priceless. I send you my deepest thanks.

To my students, who planted the idea of writing a book, I am so grateful to have you, and passing my knowledge to you is so important for me.

Thank you to the people who allowed me to include their wonderful stories in this book.

To my beautiful and wonderful wife, Erika, the past thirteen years with you by my side has been amazing; every day you've graced my life has been full of happiness. "*Je t'aimerai toujours ma chérie.*"

To my big boy, Raphaël, thank you for being so patient with Dad when he was working, even if sometimes you don't understand why so many people come to Daddy's office to play cards. You are my pride, my jewel, and I love you so much.

To my precious Mathilde, since you came into our lives two month ago, you've brought so much to our family and we love you with all our hearts, my little princess.

To my mum, Claudette, who dreamed of me before I was even born, for your support and unconditional love; you've constantly believed in me and encouraged me to be the best man possible.

To all the teachers and mentors in disguise; Spirit has sent you my way to teach me important lessons. Often, you were not even aware that you were being the instrument of Spirit—I want to thank you all.

To my guardians, angels, and muses, I've been the channel for so many inspiring pieces of art; thank you for these inspirations and ideas that seem to grow overnight in my mind.

To Schiffer Publishing, my dream was to share my passion for the Petit Lenormand with the world, and with your help this dream of mine is coming true—I want to thank you for that.

Last but not least, To Mlle Lenormand, Queen of French Cartomancy, I hope I've honored your name and title as "*La plus grande cartomancienne de France*" by my work and dedication; thank you for sending your deck my way.

Merci, Merci, Merci

ABOUT THE AUTHOR

Alexandre Musruck is internationally known for his extra-accurate readings. He is a passionate reader of oracle cards and has created numerous decks, from Tarot to Angel oracles, as well as his many attractive Lenormand decks. He has been working with the Lenormand for twenty-three years. Alexandre loves to teach people how to use their intuition, and you can find his many teaching videos and insights on his YouTube channel.

When he's not writing books, creating oracle cards, teaching audiences, or working with clients, he enjoys life on his exotic island of Réunion, a peaceful, heavenly place in the Indian Ocean, with his loving and supportive wife, Erika; his six-year-old son, Raphaël; and baby girl, Mathilde. Find more information about Alexandre at:

alexandremusruck@gmail.com
www.angelcartomancy.com
www.youtube.com/LenormandandKipperReading